H

DUBLIN INSTITUTE OF TECHNOLOGY

DUBLIN

D1357546

THE VULGARIZATION OF ART

The Victorians and Aesthetic Democracy

Victorian Literature and Culture Series

Karen Chase, Jerome J. McGann, *and* Herbert Tucker, *General Editors*

THE VULGARIZATION OF ART

The Victorians and Aesthetic Democracy

Linda Dowling

UNIVERSITY PRESS OF VIRGINIA
Charlottesville and London

THE UNIVERSITY PRESS OF VIRGINIA

First published 1996

Library of Congress Cataloging-in-Publication Data

Dowling, Linda C., 1944–
The vulgarization of art : the Victorians and aesthetic democracy / Linda Dowling.
p. cm.—(Victorian literature and culture series)
Includes bibliographical references and index.
ISBN 0-8139-1634-8 (cloth : alk. paper)
1. English literature—19th century—History and criticism—Theory, etc. 2. Art and literature—Great Britain—History—19th century. 3. Popular culture—Great Britain—History—19th century. 4. Art criticism—Great Britain—History—19th century. 5. Criticism—Great Britain—History—19th century. 6. Aesthetic movement (British art) 7. Aestheticism (Literature) 8. Aesthetics, British. 9. Arts, British. I. Title. II. Series.
PR468.A33D69 1996
820.9'357—dc20 *95-314*
CIP

Printed in the United States of America

FOR RICHARD HOWARD

I am certain only of the strong
Instinct in me (I cannot reason this)
To draw, delimit the things
I love—oh not for
Reputation or the good of others or
My own advantage, but a sort of need,
Like that for water and food.

—*1851: A Message to Denmark Hill*

Contents

Preface

"A map of the world that does not include Utopia is not worth even glancing at," wrote Oscar Wilde in *The Soul of Man under Socialism,* "for it leaves out the one country at which Humanity is always landing" (*The Artist as Critic,* 269–70). To modern readers, as to some contemporaries given to regarding Wilde as the very apostle of art for art's sake in late Victorian culture, the note of social or political engagement in such a pronouncement has seemed oddly dissonant. For while there had earlier been heard in Victorian England voices associating art with liberal or even utopian reform—the John Ruskin of *The Stones of Venice* or the Working Men's College, the William Morris of the Red House or the early years of Morris and Co.—we have been disposed to say that this association is precisely what dissolves in the turn toward pure aestheticism signaled by Walter Pater's *Studies in the History of the Renaissance.* In taking such a turn, we have also been disposed to say, Aestheticism reveals its truest nature as a denial or retreat from history.

There is a great deal in the doctrines of high Aestheticism to support such a view. To read a work like Wilde's *The Critic as Artist,* with its vision of art as a timeless reality separate from the turmoil of ordinary human existence, is today almost inevitably to suppose that the essay must be a response to Wilde's own sense of living amid a debased and fragmented modernity and in particular to what Morris, in a phrase that echoes throughout his writings, would call "the nightmare of commercial ugliness" surrounding men and women in modern England. Yet this leaves unresolved the problem of why writers like Ruskin and Morris, whose own vision of art was never less exalted than Wilde's and whose sense of living in a degraded modern landscape was, if anything, more acute and despairing, should ever have been able to imagine that art in such a situation might possess a grand power of social redemption.

There is also no question that the views of Ruskin and Morris during their respective periods of commitment to "aesthetic democracy" were those animating the leading spirits of Victorian political reform—an idea of the liberal state, as one young contributor to *Essays on Reform* would put it in 1867, as a "community ordered and bound together by affection instead of force, the desire of which is, in fact, the spring of human progress" (Goldwin Smith, 218). For the vision of social harmony and purpose implied by such an ideal is, transposed into the register of aesthetic consciousness, precisely what Ruskin had written about so unforgettably in "The Nature of Gothic," the famous chapter in *The Stones of Venice* that would inspire so many younger Victorian readers. Among them was Morris, in whom traces of what might be called his earlier aesthetic activism would linger even into the disenchantment of his later years. For Morris's grand object, a friend would later conclude, had been "none other than the democratisation of beauty" (Compton-Rickett, 21).

We have been reluctant to take such claims seriously, I think, because of a certain tendency in contemporary criticism to regard the very idea of the aesthetic as mystification, to see all talk of art or beauty as no more than one of the ruses or stratagems through which societies perpetuate themselves as orders of domination. At the level of theory, this has given us works like Peter Bürger's *Theory of the Avant-Garde* or Pierre Bourdieu's *Distinction.* At the level of practical criticism, it has produced in recent years innumerable articles and studies like—to choose an example virtually at random—Martha Woodmansee's *The Author, Art, and the Market,* in which the study of the aesthetic is dismissed at the outset ("great minds speaking with one another over and above the historical process," 7) to proceed with the more pressing business at hand: uncovering "the underlying motives" (5) of writers or artists as revealed by their "professional and economic interests" (8), thereby illustrating "the more fundamental material impulses" (20) that are the hidden and unlovely truth of any work of literature, philosophy, or art.

At the same time, there may be heard in contemporary criticism a number of voices that, while always insisting in the strongest terms on the historicity of the work of art, have insisted as well that taking history seriously means taking with equal seriousness the power of social redemption that writers like Ruskin and Morris were ready to attribute to the aesthetic. Thus, for instance, Fredric Jameson has spoken of aesthetic experience as offering to the imagination a vision of meaning or significance so total that the real world, in intolerable contrast to it, "stands condemned," thus opening the moment in which "the Utopian idea, the revolutionary blueprint, may be conceived" (90). In the same way, George Levine has insisted in a recent essay that "what great art does through its form is both compose and reflect community" (21), and Terry Eagleton, in *The Ideology of the Aesthetic,* has made a point of reminding his readers of the enormous influence exerted on Karl Marx by Friedrich Schiller's ideal of wholly realized human development in his *On the Aesthetic Education of Man, in a Series of Letters.*

In Eagleton, concerned as he is with the relation between aesthetic theory and the emergence of revolutionary socialism, one comes very close to the perspective needed to understand Ruskin and Morris in their own cultural moment. In the later nineteenth century a work like *The Stones of Venice,* with its luminous picture of a Gothic world in which labor and prayer and play belonged to an as yet unfragmented communal reality, had the power to transform the lives of Victorian readers. For the metaphysics of community on which such an image draws, in Ruskin's case through the "Common Sense" and "civil society" theories of the Scottish Enlightenment as well as through reading Schiller, is that of Schiller's "aesthetic state": the ideal polity, where "taste leads knowledge out into the broad daylight of Common Sense [*Gemeinsinn*], and transforms a monopoly of the Schools into the common possession [*Gemeingut*] of Human Society as a whole" (*Aesthetic Education,* 217). This is the image of social harmony and human self-realization, as Eagleton reminds us, that would leave so lasting an impression on Marx.

To some Victorian readers, by the same token, an identical impulse toward restored community seemed evident even in Pater's *Studies in the History of the Renaissance,* which is today normally taken as the manifesto of the Aestheticist withdrawal into art. For like Ruskin and Morris before him, as John Morley would argue in the *Fortnightly Review,* Pater is motivated by a "craving for the infusion of something harmonious and beautiful about the bare lines of daily living" ("Mr. Pater's Essays," 476), which is simply another way of describing the liberal spirit in Victorian culture. Morley was himself an eloquent spokesman for Victorian liberalism, but just the same point would be made from the opposing perspective by W. J. Courthope, whose indignantly clairvoyant Toryism so often led him to see connections hidden from modern view. "What at first sight appears the unnatural connection between the doctrines of Mr. Ruskin and the school of the Modern Renaissance," says Courthope, meaning Pater and those under his influence, ceases to be unnatural in the moment one has identified the strain of "literary Liberalism" that is their common denominator ("Modern Culture," 409).

The same strain of literary liberalism, as Courthope instantly would have recognized, lies behind Wilde's remarks on utopia in *The Soul of Man under Socialism.* Yet we are not mistaken, for all that, in seeing in Pater's *Renaissance* a withdrawal from politics or history into art or in catching in *The Critic as Artist* overtones of Wilde's own sense that, in an age of overwhelming vulgarity, those who devote themselves to literature and music and art constitute a fugitive elite, the last guardians of the spirit of beauty in a nightmare landscape of modern ugliness. This is why one so often has a sense, while reading *The Soul of Man under Socialism,* of Wilde's aesthetic liberalism collapsing inward upon some unseen paradox lying at its center, so that every gesture in the direction of social redemption is immediately undermined by an urgent awareness that art, if it is to survive in the modern age, must be isolated or protected from the hideousness of mass society. "Art should never try to be popular," Wilde is moved to declare at one point. "The public should try to make itself artistic" (247).

The unseen paradox that explains Wilde's impatience at such moments, I shall argue in the following chapters, is this: at the heart of the vision of aesthetic democracy inspiring Ruskin and Morris, one still evident in Wilde's musings on mankind and utopia, lies an ideal of aristocratic sensibility unrecognized as such, something very nearly resembling Friedrich Nietzsche's *seelische-vornehm* (aristocratic in soul or spirit) as the hidden source of value in moral and aesthetic terms. On a purely logical or semantic level, the collapse that had threatened aesthetic democracy from the very beginning is the loss or emptying out of meaning that occurs in any context where "noble" or "aristocratic" is no longer permitted to function in relation to a set of terms—the ignoble, the vulgar, the base—in opposition to which it had originally assumed its meaning. So far as the idea of aesthetic democracy had unconsciously implied for Ruskin or Morris an "aristocracy of everyone," as the title of a recent book innocently phrases it, the paradox is then what comes to exert a nearly intolerable pressure on the Wilde who speaks in *The Soul of Man under Socialism.*

The paradox of aesthetic democracy in this same form was

glimpsed by Ruskin only toward the end of his career. It would never be felt as such by Morris, for whom the notion of taste as an expression of aristocratic sensibility, beyond the reach of the teeming masses, would remain the repressed element in his desire for social transformation. Yet we cannot make sense of Ruskin or Morris, it seems to me, either in the shape of their careers or in their drifting toward a final disenchantment, without taking the precise measure of such repression to mind and spirit, trying to see, as they could not, the deeper sense in which the project of aesthetic democracy had been from the very beginning at odds with itself. By the same token, I think that we only understand Pater's emergent and Wilde's wholly developed aesthetic elitism when we have seen its relation to a suddenly perceived need to rescue art from the degradations of a mass society—Morris's nightmare landscape of modern ugliness now glimpsed as history itself.

The aristocratic disdain for bourgeois morality displayed by a character like Lord Henry Wotton in Wilde's *The Picture of Dorian Gray* is, on this account, simply the return to visibility of the very element so long repressed in the project of aesthetic democracy as conceived by Ruskin or Morris, the lingering trace of an older world of divine right, natural law, and preordained rank or status wholly inconsistent with newer ideas of equality and popular sovereignty. I will argue that this anomalous or paradoxical element did not simply play a fundamental role in the program of aesthetic democracy from the beginning—that it was already there in phantasmic form, for instance, in the medievalism of Ruskin and Morris and only became more visible in Pater and Wilde—but that it did so for a particular reason: nearly two centuries before, at the very moment when the Whig polity had been urgently seeking alternatives to absolutist rule as the basis of its own legitimation, a Whig nobleman had devised a theory in which that basis was provided by the instantaneous and universal power of aesthetic perception.

The moment in question is the period following the Glorious Revolution in England, when the contract theory set out in John Locke's second treatise of government would, while providing a practical rationale for the new order represented by William and Mary and the Bill of Rights, leave it without any clear basis in any transcendental value. The Whig nobleman was Locke's pupil, Anthony Ashley Cooper, third earl of Shaftesbury, whose *Characteristics of Men, Manners, Opinions, Times, Etc.,* though little read through most of the three centuries separating his time from our own, developed a theory of the moral sense—an ability to tell right from wrong innate to and universal among human beings—that would have a profound influence on all subsequent writing in both moral and political philosophy. The paradox of aesthetic democracy, as I shall attempt to trace its consequences in the following pages, originates in the moment when Lord Shaftesbury, raised as an English nobleman among paintings, music, and the Greek and Roman classics, is led by certain implications of his own argument to imagine that his own deep appreciation of these things must be, if only latently or potentially, basic to human nature itself.

The earliest version of this book was written in Madrid in the academic year 1992–93; the present version was written in Bellagio in the summer 1994. I would like to thank those in both places whose support made the task of writing in unfamiliar surroundings immeasurably easier: in Madrid, Lorenzo Rodríguez of the Asociación J. William Fulbright, Patricia Zahniser of the Comisión de Intercambio Cultural, and, most especially, my friends Gema Chocano Díaz and Victor Santiago Menéndez Martínez; at Bellagio, Pasquale Pesce, Gianna Celli, Elena Ongania, and Linda Triangolo of the Rockefeller Foundation. In addition, conversations with a number of the other fellows at the Bellagio Study Center—Sir Henry Chadwick, Christopher Dow, Alan Eyre, Katalin Gönczöl, Ian Holford, Shi-ye Li, Aharon Oppenheimer, and László Valki—influenced the direction of the argument as it now stands.

At home, conversations with Stefan Collini, Gertrude Himmelfarb, George Levine, Dorothy Thompson, Hugh Witemeyer, and Susan Wolfson have at various points given shape to my thinking about aesthetic democracy. Herbert Tucker and Elizabeth Helsinger read the latest version of the manuscript with a critical eye and made useful suggestions for revision. Finally, since *The Vulgarization of Art* was conceived as the prelude to a related and subsequent project, a study of Charles Eliot Norton and aesthetic democracy in the far different context of late-nineteenth-century America, I should like to thank Quentin Anderson, Chandos Brown, William Dowling, and Jackson Lears, whose conversation has done so much to keep me attentive to the transatlantic implications of my argument.

THE VULGARIZATION OF ART

The Victorians and Aesthetic Democracy

The man in the street, finding no worth in himself which corresponds to the force which built a tower or sculptured a marble god, feels poor when he looks on these. To him a palace, a statue, or a costly book have an alien and forbidding air, much like a gay equipage, and seem to say like that, "Who are you, sir?" Yet they are all his, suitors for his notice, petitioners to his faculties that they will come out and take possession. The picture waits for my verdict: it is not to commend me, but I am to settle its claims to praise.

—*Emerson,* Self-Reliance

I

Victorian Liberalism and Aesthetic Democracy

We must encourage all efforts to vulgarise *a sense of beauty.* (*Fortnightly Review*)

THE GREAT SIGNIFICANCE of the Hyde Park riots of July 1866, it is sometimes said, is less that they prompted the House of Commons to pass the Second Reform Bill than that they prompted Matthew Arnold to write *Culture and Anarchy* (1869). Drawn to the balcony of his house in Chester Square in the middle of the night, Arnold watched as an angry mob of what the *Times* of London called "roughs" ("the usual slouching, shambling man-boys who constitute the mass of the ordinary London multitude" [24 July 1866, 9]) stoned the windows of his neighbor, the commissioner of police. As he meditated upon these scenes, Arnold would come to see them as nothing less than the outward sign of a deeper anarchy, the reckless moral disorder born of "the assertion of personal liberty" as the "central idea of English life and politics"—the vehemently asserted right of everyone in England of "Doing As One Likes" (*Culture and Anarchy,* 117). This avidity for personal liberty, Arnold concluded, this political "libertinism," represented an anarchy bred within political liberalism itself.

The publication of *Culture and Anarchy* has been taken to mark the symbolic moment when an early Victorian concern with political reform and social criticism, the world of the Chartists, Thomas Hood's "Song of the Shirt," or Charles Dickens's *Hard Times,* began to shift toward a late-Victorian concern with aesthetic criticism and imaginative release, the world represented by Walter Pater's *Renaissance,* the Metaphysical Society, or H. Rider Haggard's *She.* Thus, for instance, Catherine Gallagher in *The Industrial Reformation of English Fiction* sees Arnold's turn toward a "politics of culture," with its emphasis on an autonomous, "disinterested" sphere of art and literature, as disarming a whole tradition of social criticism and bringing the "Condition of England" debate to a close (264). The Aesthetic Movement of 1865–95 has long been regarded, by the same token, as constituting the central episode of this late Victorian flight from politics, and even within Aestheticism, degrees of sociopolitical engagement have been made to serve as a principle of critical differentiation. Consequently, it has become conventional to distinguish between the "Art for Life's Sake" projects of John Ruskin and William Morris and the "Art for Art's Sake" experiments of Pater and Oscar Wilde.

To contemporary observers, however, especially those unsympathetic to the notion of radical social change, the Aesthetic Movement appeared in an altogether different light. Thus, to W. J. Courthope, as we have heard, the Pater of the *Renaissance* seems no less than Ruskin a representative of "literary Liberalism," a program carrying over into aesthetic theory the same egalitarian impulses so obviously at work in the movement for Victorian political reform. Yet Courthope, for whom the French Revolution in its moment of Jacobin excess was the source of all modern radicalism, was in no position to see that the liberalism he correctly glimpses in Pater's otherwise disengaged Aestheticism has its real roots in an older body of eighteenth-century moral and aesthetic theory and in particular in the assumption that the capacity to respond to beauty is universal, shared by all human beings, as the young Edmund Burke had said in his *Philosophical Enquiry into the Origin of Our Ideas of the Sublime and the Beautiful,* "high and low, learned and unlearned" (104).

In the immediate background of Burke's aesthetic theory, in turn, lies the *Characteristics* of the third earl of Shaftesbury, whose own theory of the *sensus communis,* normally thought of as belonging to moral philosophy, had in fact emerged in response to a sense of political or historical crisis uncannily like that of Arnold in *Culture and Anarchy.* The resemblance is not accidental, for *Culture and Anarchy* is the great Victorian expression of an idea that had originated with Shaftesbury in the period of political demoralization following the Glorious Revolution of 1688, the beginning of what I shall be calling the tradition of Whig aesthetics. This resemblance was immediately evident, for instance to Leslie Stephen, whose unrivaled knowledge of eighteenth-century thought made clear to him the analogy with the Victorian present. "Lord Shaftesbury," observed Stephen in 1873, looking for a way to make the eighteenth century comprehensible to readers of *Fraser's Magazine,* was the "Matthew Arnold of Queen Anne's reign" (81).

The resemblance Stephen sees here concerns at bottom the question of how legitimacy is to be achieved in the liberal polity, how a state that derives its authority from the consent of its people may pretend to be founded upon anything more secure than—as its enemies kept warning—the restless, irrational impulses and appetites of an ignorant populace. The answer, for both Shaftesbury and Arnold, would lie in what Arnold famously called "Culture," which consists less of mere education than of induction into a polis of the mind or spirit where people become, through a lived experience of art, literature, and ideas, the better selves that had before lain undeveloped due to the accidents of social circumstance. To understand the vision of culture at the center of *Culture and Anarchy* is in this sense to have grasped not simply the theory of the *sensus communis* in which it has its deepest roots but also the entire tradition of Whig aesthetics that originates in Shaftesbury's *Characteristics*.

In recent years we have begun to recover some sense of Shaftesbury as a moral philosopher immensely important in his own time and of his *Characteristics* (1711) as a seminal work lying in the immediate background of Humean epistemology, Kantian aesthetics, and, more unexpectedly, the economic theory of Adam Smith. More recently still, a view of the *Characteristics* considered as a sort of handbook for bourgeois subjectivity—especially the rhapsodically elevated, quasi-Platonic dialogue entitled *The Moralists*—has led such commentators as Terry Eagleton to see in the "genially aristocratic" Shaftesbury an "eloquent spokesman" for "the bourgeois public sphere of eighteenth-century England" (36, 35).[1]

It is, however, only in Shaftesbury's less public and finished works—the journal entries known as the *Philosophical Regimen,* the rough notes for a treatise on the fine arts known as *Second Characters*—that the raw historical forces out of which the idealist rhapsodies of *The Moralists* would so unexpectedly be fashioned become visible. For only these relatively unpolished works provide a glimpse of Shaftesbury's personal, existential crisis as he faces his own radical anomalousness—an English nobleman living after the historical epoch that had witnessed the execution of one king (1649), the expulsion of another (1688), and the abolition of the House of Lords (1649). "Why do I cumber the ground?" Shaftesbury bitterly asks himself in the pages of this journal. "Why live below my order and species, degenerate, worthless, productive of nothing good, . . . a briar and worse than a briar, a fungus, an excrescence, a disease of the earth?" (*Life,* 145–46).[2]

Thrust by the tumultuous events of the first English revolution of 1641–59 from a traditional social system rooted in status and custom, nobles like Shaftesbury found themselves inhabiting a world in which the ontological conditions of English nobility had been forever altered. Instead of living within a social hierarchy where it was assumed, as Charles Taylor has said, that "man could only be himself in relation to a cosmic order" and that "the state claimed to body forth this order and hence to be one of men's principal channels of contact with it" (*Hegel,* 410), Shaftesbury awoke to a world in which the "Restoration" of the outward semblance of traditional forms in 1660—the monarchy, titles of nobility, the House of Lords—could neither disguise the ontological rupture forced by the English revolution nor guarantee that such events would not occur again. Henceforth it would be impossible for nobles to inhabit an aristocratic *Lebensform* regarded in the old, pre-seventeenth-century way as altogether natural, normative, and unproblematic.

Such nobles as Shaftesbury, whose family had risen to power and eminence on the dangerously volatile currents of the Restoration, would thereafter occupy a sphere of contingency and human construction where their status, titles, and house of assembly could conceivably be abolished anew, where the nobles recognized themselves at a deep level as now serving on the suffrance of the people. In this context, Shaftesbury's anguished sense of self-division and personal anomaly demands to be understood as a response to historical flux and dispossession, Shaftesbury experiencing the nightmare of history in almost painfully literal terms, as when he writes in his journal, "Dreams, dreams.—A dark night; dead sleep; starts; disturbing visions; faint endeavours to awake.—A Sick reason; labyrinth; wood; sea.—Waves tossing; billows surging; the driving of the wreck; giddy whirlwinds; eddies; and the overwhelming gulf" (*Life,* 124).

The more tormented entries of Shaftesbury's journal represent in this sense a sudden, anguished sense of history gone meaningless, of a world of rapid and incomprehensible change in which the old landmarks have either become dangerous or have disappeared entirely. All Shaftesbury's stylistic polish and "aristocratic geniality," then, must be understood as having been thrown up over an abyss—an "overwhelming gulf"—a deep sense of deracination and self-mistrust that would erupt in the collapses of body and spirit he suffered in 1698 and again in 1703 and would persist in his acute and continuing sense of his own radical insubstantiality as man and nobleman, living on in a world where the withdrawal of public consent or belief in aristocratic privilege has transformed noblemen themselves into unreal shadow figures on the stage of history. "Behold," as Shaftesbury tells himself upon succeeding to the title in 1699, "thou art become an appendix to a grange! An appurtenance to an estate and title!" (*Life,* 127).

Shaftesbury suffers the trauma of vast historical change and dispossession on especially painful terms because he experiences it as a dilemma of divided loyalties. Both of the two central figures of his family circle—his grandfather, the first earl of Shaftesbury, and his tutor, John Locke—had been intimately involved in producing the new postrevolutionary sociopolitical order in England. Immortalized as the satanic figure of Achitophel in John Dryden's famous poem, his grandfather had grasped with an extraordinary clarity the possibility of founding the legitimacy of a Whig polity upon the principle of popular consent as represented by the sovereignty of Parliament. Almost uniquely among members of his class, the first earl had penetrated the local politics of the Exclusion Crisis to an understanding of the irreversible historical processes that were bringing new individualist energies to the fore. The first earl would be remembered during the lifetime of his grandson, however, in precisely the terms he had been viewed by Dryden and the Court party at the time of the Exclusion Crisis he had so boldly sought to foment—as a rabble-rouser and demagogue, an unprincipled schemer interested in nothing more exalted than his own power, a traitor to his king and rank.

In the earlier, prerevolutionary world of communal ties and unproblematic hierarchies, Shaftesbury's feeling for his grandfather might have been a matter of simple familial loyalty or dynastic pride. In the post-revolutionary moment, by contrast, Shaftesbury's persistent effort "to vindicate the much-injured memory of one who [was] a champion in that cause" (*Life,* 325) was to become a larger defense of the Whig political revolution itself—of "the Cause," as Shaftesbury would ever simply and grandly refer to it. The third earl would thus devote his short lifetime to vindicating his grandfather's imperfectly glimpsed vision of a Whig or liberal polity—that alternative order to autocracy in which the authority of those appointed to govern the polity would in some sense flow from the consent of those over whose lives and fortunes they had been granted control, "all sharers (though at so far a distance from each other)," as Shaftesbury declared, "in the government of themselves" (*Second Characters,* 22). Yet even as he defended them, Shaftesbury always sensed on some deeper level that his loyalty to his grandfather and to "the Cause" to which Locke, had given extraordinary philosophical substantiality in the *Two Treatises of Government* (1690)[3] was silently bringing forth a new sociopolitical order in which the very possibility of traditional loyalties and customary ties would be forever changed.

Shaftesbury thus came to perceive Locke as simultaneously the theorist of the political cause to which he owed his deepest loyalty and the theorist of an emergent new moral disposition to which Shaftesbury found himself responding with resistance and dread. As the author of the *Two Treatises,* Locke was widely considered to have destroyed the arguments of the divine-right apologists as they had been put forward by their most notable defender, Sir Robert Filmer in *Patriarcha* (1680). Yet Shaftesbury came to believe that Locke—despite his supremely successful dismantling of Filmer's argument from biblical scripture for patriarchal autocracy in the first treatise—had deeply blundered in the second treatise when he tried to make the positive case for the Whig consensual polity.[4]

Here lies the grave dilemma, as Peter Laslett has ably demonstrated, born of Locke's success in disposing of Filmer's argument for absolutism. For if revealed religion and biblical scripture are removed as the basis of the just state, what else will provide its ground in anything more transient and arbitrary than mere social convention? Locke's problem here—the problem of the liberal polity as it would persist over the next two hundred years—is further complicated by his own revolutionary contributions to the theory of knowledge. The consensual polity as sketched by Locke in the *Two Treatises* can scarcely do without the epistemology propounded in his *Essay Concerning Human Understanding* (1690), because in the implications of radical equality contained in the doctrine of the tabula rasa—the idea that mind or consciousness begins in everyone as a blank slate written upon by the world—there lies the most fundamental justification of such a polity.

The epistemology of the *Essay* is by this means always able to invoke in political terms the Whig principle of *isonomia* (equal treatment under law) that Locke himself, as J. G. A. Pocock has noted, had absorbed from Stoic philosophy and the classical republican tradition, the idea that men are "equal by nature, in the sense that all men are born equipped with the same capacities" (*Machiavellian Moment,* 473). This notion of shared capacities—for sensation, introspection, and scarcely anything beyond them—as much as the manner in which Locke's attack on innate ideas operated to discredit older theories of divine right explains why some version of Lockean epistemology must be retained by any truly persuasive theory of the Whig or liberal state.

To stake the defense of the Whig polity here, however, was in Shaftesbury's view silently to subscribe to a notion of a merely external morality, of a human nature driven by a narrow self-interest, of the impossibility of any nobler springs of action. At precisely this point, Shaftesbury's instinctive loyalty both to the older ethical disposition that Michael Oakeshott termed the morality of communal ties and to the ancient metaphysical order that Charles Taylor calls the ontic logos would reassert itself in dissent. "According to Mr. Locke," as Shaftesbury wrote indignantly to a young friend residing in Oxford, virtue has "no other measure, law, or rule, than fashion and custom. . . . And thus neither right nor wrong, virtue nor vice, are anything in themselves; nor is there any trace or idea of them naturally imprinted on human minds" (*Life,* 404). In Shaftesbury's eyes, Locke had thus sunk below even the notoriously cynical estimate of human moral capacities advanced by Thomas Hobbes: "It was Mr. Locke that struck the home blow: for Mr. Hobbes's character and base slavish principles in government took off the poison of his philosophy. 'Twas Mr. Locke that struck at all fundamentals, threw all order and virtue out of the world, and made the very ideas of these (which are the same as those of God) *unnatural,* and without foundation in our minds" (*Life,* 403).

In this moment of acute moral analysis, Shaftesbury at once recognized the political implications for "the Cause" of an individualist ethic grounded solely in selfish or prudential considerations and himself felt the desiccating insufficiency of the individualist ethic in all the deeper purposes of life. For by the turn of the eighteenth century, the morality of communal ties was fading in England, disappearing with the communal circumstances of life in English agricultural villages. Forced by his grandfather's cause and his tutor's epistemological revolution into the starker realm of individualist modernity, Shaftesbury nonetheless felt the claim of this immemorially older, stabler form of life. On the pages of the same diary that preserves his anguished self-consciousness as an isolated individual, Shaftesbury recorded his complex dealings with "my family," meaning by this term the dense network of retainers and dependents, unrelated to him by blood, that connected him to the earlier world of communal ties. "Communal in character and customary in inspiration," as Oakeshott characterized it, in this traditional world "the self-knowledge of each member is the knowledge of himself *as a member*" and "the good" is always recognized "as the common good of the society—of the family or of the village community" (19; emphasis added).

In the same moment that Shaftesbury experienced the alienating burden and isolation of the new individualist disposition, he perceived that Locke's epistemological attack on "all fundamentals" had unwittingly aided precisely his grandfather's enemies, the enemies of "the Cause." For even at the moment when they were left behind by history at the level of events, those voices continuing to defend the supremacy of the throne over the commons quite evidently retained a deeper ideological resource: they have remained in communication with an ideal world equally vital to the social functioning of human beings. This realm of the ontic logos, as Taylor has termed it in *Sources of the Self* (161), constitutes that meaningful order of timeless or transcendent values in which the moral existence of specific individuals and historical societies may find its ground.

When he denounced Locke's assault on "all fundamentals," then, Shaftesbury grasped that the power of any such apology for monarchical supremacy as Filmer's derived in the last analysis not from any of Filmer's local arguments but from the metaphysics entailed by them: an ideal and wholly meaningful cosmic order in which God and monarchy and family, loyalty to one's parents, and honesty or virtue in one's relations with others are interconnected and inseparable. To give up any element of this system of the ontic logos, either in the name of political convenience or newly contrived theories of popular consent, is to be set adrift in a world unmoored from any basis in the transcendent realm; it is to exist as a hand severed from the body.

As Shaftesbury recognizes, the partisans of divine-right sovereignty lay claim to a transcendental legitimacy for their polity without which the Whig polity, founded on the principle of popular consent, would always be made to appear as nothing more than a cynical mechanism operated by such knaves as Achitophel to control the dangerous energies of fools. The "zealots for despotic power" vilifying his grandfather as Achitophel (*Life,* xix) had in this sense won the ideological war, even if they had undoubtedly lost the political battle represented by the Glorious Revolution of 1688. In this moment of ideological analysis and moral dissent, Shaftesbury would invent the moral-aesthetic sense as the solution to his dilemma of divided loyalties.

Shaftesbury's task thus becomes to recover a principle adequate to the moral justification of the Whig polity.[5] Given Locke's epistemological revolution, this principle must be seen to retain its intelligibility in the new universe of empiricism, for Locke's attack on innate ideas and Cambridge Platonism had forever banished the possibility of any direct appeal to a transcendent order of virtue and beauty.[6] This is the context in which Locke's own repeated appeals to an unspecified law of nature somehow "writ in the hearts of all mankind" (*Two Treatises,* 274) would seem even to sympathetic readers singularly empty or hollow, so at odds did it appear to be with Locke's own ban on innate ideas in the *Essay.*[7]

Thus, Shaftesbury's argument for a moral order intrinsic to human experience comes to be expressed in the famous doctrine of the "natural moral sense" (*Characteristics,* 1:262). In Locke's epistemology, the immediacy of ideas derived from the senses gives them their primacy, the notion that the things seen, touched, or heard have a kind of natural priority in the order of experience that makes them, in the *Essay Concerning Human Understanding,* the raw stuff of our perception. Shaftesbury's moral sense, then, must operate as do the five physical senses in the empirical world of sensory data, registering ethical impressions with all the immediacy and vividness of the taste of salt upon the tongue or the touch of fire upon the skin. As it responds to the world through its moral sense, the mind, declares Shaftesbury, "feels the soft and harsh, the agreeable and disagreeable in the affections" (*Characteristics,* 1:251).

By accepting the terms of Locke's epistemological revolution in this way—the primacy of sensations, the rejection of innate ideas and of the teleological conception of human nature—Shaftesbury remained loyal to the new sociopolitical order of individualism that his grandfather and tutor had ushered into English national life. By dissenting from Locke's prudential morality and his implicit (if unwitting) attack upon "all fundamentals . . . all order and virtue," however, Shaftesbury simultaneously registered his loyalty to the older order of the ontic logos. This underlying and unrenounced loyalty appeared whenever Shaftesbury in the course of his Whig apologetics adopted the vocabulary of philosophical and religious Platonism and appealed for example, to *to kalon*—

the idea of the true, the good and the beautiful understood as a reciprocal whole: "What is harmonious and proportionable," as his spokesman declares in *The Moralists,* "is true; and what is at once both beautiful and true is, of consequence, agreeable and good" (*Characteristics,* 2:268–69).

Even as Shaftesbury struggled to relocate what he believed to be the innate and disinterested human moral capacity to the newly shrunken realm required by Locke's epistemological revolution, then, he continually strived to invest that realm with the larger dimensions of the older transcendental order of the ontic logos. Repeatedly grappling with such ruinous modern philosophers as Locke and Hobbes, whom he sees as declaring, "Beauty is nothing.—Virtue is nothing," as well as battling Hobbes's and Locke's equivalents in the sphere of the arts—those "anti-virtuosi" who declare, "perspective [is] nothing.—Music [is] nothing," Shaftesbury, invoking the tradition of philosophical and religious transcendentalism running back through the Cambridge Platonists to Plotinus and Plato in antiquity, would always insistently protest, "But these are the greatest realities of things, especially the beauty and order of [the] affections" (*Second Characters,* 178).

In the same way, Shaftesbury would continually turn back to the ethical resources available within the classical-republican and Stoic traditions. For here he found the presumption of a natural sociability—"the social hypothesis," as he called it in his journal (*Life,* 415)—with which to buttress the crumbling old morality of communal ties and to moderate the effects of the withering individualism being bred out of the new Whig contractual state. Throughout the essays of *Characteristics,* Shaftesbury labored to portray the moral-aesthetic sense itself as a *sensus communis*—a sense, as he put it in his essay of the same name, "of public weal, and of the common interest; love of the community or society, natural affection, humanity, obligingness, or that sort of civility which rises from a just sense of the common rights of mankind" (1:70). In the classical-republican and Stoic idea of an irreducibly social world existing as the prior condition and ground for the noble realization of any individual life, Shaftesbury located both the idea that bestowed upon republican political life its deeper reason for being and the presumption that stood in such devastating contrast to English political life as it was conducted "after the way of our Whig-grandees," intent merely on their "fashionable companionships, long suppers, and sittings-up" (*Life,* 463).

This is the irreducibly social and moral dimension of human life—what we have heard Shaftesbury call "the greatest realities of things"—that Locke's philosophical analysis, in Shaftesbury's view, had left so wholly out of account as to jeopardize the very Whig political order that Locke himself had helped to establish. For Locke had seemingly abandoned the great burden assumed by any political theory appealing to popular consent as the basis of civic authority: the task of showing that the citizenry is not a mere seething mass of irrational or egocentric desire. Instead of defending the central Whig premise that virtue, reason, and disinterestedness might be safely presumed in ordinary men, Locke seemed to fall back on some mere law of opinion or custom to regulate the polity and, at a somewhat greater remove, on a mysteriously unspecific law supposed to be "writ in the hearts of all mankind."

So long as Locke, with his banishment of innate ideas and the teleological essence of man, could do no better than to ground moral rectitude in the commandments of a God with power to enforce them, as he had said, "by rewards and punishments, of infinite weight and duration, in another life" (*Essay,* 352), this mere "rod and sweetmeat" theory of moral action, as Shaftesbury so contemptuously called it (*Characteristics,* 2:41), would ever implicitly but devastatingly concede the persistent Tory charge that Whig "liberty" was nothing more than a mask for licentiousness and libertinism.[8] So long as Whigs like Locke embraced Hobbesian notions of self-interest and external morality, Dryden's horrific vision of "the dregs of a democracy" presided over by Achitophel would continue to haunt the English political horizon.

When Shaftesbury roused himself to oppose "my old tutor and governor," he expressed his dissent under the cover of a critique of Locke for having exposed the Whig cause to potential delegitimation at the hands of its enemies. As Shaftesbury located in the moral sense a principle adequate to the moral justification of the Whig polity against these enemies, however, he simultaneously registered his divided loyalty to the ontic logos and the morality of communal ties. For with the notion of a "natural moral sense," Shaftesbury invested Plato's *to kalon* with the immediacy of sensory impressions and, hence, with all the authority of Locke's epistemological revolution. At the same time, he imparted to the "impressions" of the moral sense all the ethical depth of the Stoics' natural sociability doctrine and all the metaphysical authority of the ontic logos.

In this moment, Shaftesbury found himself in precisely the philosophical position Alasdair MacIntyre describes in *After Virtue.* For the explicit rejection by Locke and Hobbes of the traditional Aristotelian ideas concerning the essential nature and telos of human beings makes it henceforth impossible "to supply anything like a traditional account or justification of the virtues." Yet the virtues were no less necessary—indeed, were more necessary—at the end of the seventeenth century than they had ever been. How could they be recaptured for ordinary social life as well as for the Whig polity that now had to take that social life for its ground? Henceforth it would be necessary, MacIntyre concludes, to understand the virtues either "as expressions of the natural passions of the individual" (the path Shaftesbury followed with his notions of natural benevolence and the natural moral sense) or "as dispositions necessary to curb and to limit the destructive effect of some of those same natural passions" (228) (the path to be taken by Bernard Mandeville and David Hume).

Yet there remains a sense in which Shaftesbury's struggle to reconcile the competing claims of the empiricist and the ontic orders in the interest of legitimating the Whig cause produced as an unintended consequence something entirely new: the aesthetic sense and, more generally, philosophical aesthetics. For when Shaftesbury declared that the mind "feels the soft and harsh, the agreeable and disagreeable in the affections," he went on to insist that it did so because the moral sense operated like a connoisseur's taste in the fine arts and found "a foul and fair, a harmonious and a dissonant, as really and truly here as in any musical numbers or in the outward forms or representations of sensible things (*Characteristics,* 1:251).[9] Modeling the operation of the moral sense after the responses of virtuoso taste or *goût,* Shaftesbury may thus be seen unconsciously assuming as his model the spontaneity, decisiveness, and unanimity in artistic judgments characteristic of the homogeneous circles of aristocratic and gentry amateurs in which he himself participated with such distinction: "*No sooner* the eye opens upon figures, the ear to sounds, *than straight* the beautiful results and grace and harmony are known and acknowledged" (2:137; emphasis added).

"No sooner are actions viewed," as Shaftesbury then says of the moral sense, "than straight an inward eye distinguishes, and sees the fair and shapely, the amiable and admirable, apart from the deformed, the foul, the odious, or the despicable" (2:137). The great significance to Shaftesbury of this analogy between the operation of the moral sense and the responses of virtuoso taste or *gusto,* however, is the possibility of providing, as Locke could not, a moral justification for the liberal polity and its claim that humanity, as Shaftesbury declared, "is indeed improved and raised by free Government" (*Original Letters of John Locke, Algernon Sidney, and Lord Shaftesbury,* 193). In this context Shaftesbury typically deployed the aesthetic analogy to assert the real existence in human life of disinterested moral action, virtue as a quality of actions performed not in hopes of any reward, immediate or distant, but simply and purely out of a love for virtue. This is precisely where Locke, as we have heard Shaftesbury say, had most signally failed to provide an account of ordinary human beings as having any innate capacity for virtuous action, having been able in the *Essay* to come up with nothing better than the "rod and sweetmeat" theory of divine rewards and punishments.

For this reason, despite its enormous subsequent importance in the development of philosophical aesthetics, Shaftesbury's aesthetic analogy functions most significantly in the *Characteristics* as a model of disinterested response, keeping before his readers an idea of pleasure in beauty as an end in itself that will serve to put Shaftesbury's account of virtue or goodness beyond the reach of the Hobbesian claim that genuine disinterestedness is always, when we uncover the secret springs of human action, an illusion. Shaftesbury will insist on the disinterestedness of the aesthetic response, and he will do so as a matter of simple intelligibility. He understood the pleasure gained from beautiful art or nature as serving no other end than its own delight. Thus, while it may make sense in Hobbesian terms to imagine someone going to a concert or even pretending to enjoy a concert out of some motive of self-interest—to impress a patron, perhaps, or to gain entrance to a social circle—the idea that anyone could actually experience enjoyment in return for a reward remains even in empiricist terms unintelligible.

With this account of the disinterestedness of the moral-aesthetic sense disarming both Hobbes's egoistic and Locke's prudential versions of human moral action, the way is clear for Shaftesbury to attribute such a moral capacity to the full range of English political subjects. "The natural equality there is among those of the same species," as he expresses the idea of *isonomia* (*Characteristics,* 1:70), Shaftesbury now shows to be completed by a moral equality underlying all the outward differences of station, education, and rank among Englishmen. For if, as he declares, the man "of thorough good breeding" is "incapable of doing a rude or brutal action" (1:86), so too does the "ordinary" or "common" man, who "gives no other answer to the thought of villainy than that he cannot possibly find in his heart to set about it, or conquer the natural aversion he has to it" (1:88). Thus, as Shaftesbury argues for the equality of moral capacity among all ranks, he simultaneously opens the way for the aesthetic sense, arising as a logical entailment of the moral sense in later-eighteenth-century aesthetic theory, to be attributed in turn to all persons.[10] Burke's *Enquiry,* where "the pleasure of all the senses" is "the same in all, high and low, learned and unlearned" (104), and Immanuel Kant's *Critique of Judgment,* where taste becomes "a sense common to all mankind" (227), now lie just below the horizon.[11]

By demonstrating in the compelling terms provided by the aesthetic analogy the capacity for disinterested response within every Englishman, then, Shaftesbury was triumphantly able to vindicate the fundamental premise of the Whig polity that a state founded upon the principle of popular consent does not require the cosmic authoritarianism of divine-right rule for its own authority but may instead safely rely on the judgment of ordinary citizens, "all sharers," as we have heard him say, "in the government of themselves." In the new, post-Lockean world of self-dependent subjects and consensual states, such a polity must of necessity stake its claim to legitimacy on the immanent order of humankind, once the transcendental hierarchies of the ontic logos have been so decisively canceled by history. In a world cut off from the older certitudes of divine law, this new and largely secular notion of the moral-aesthetic sense as implying a universal moral capacity will continuously operate to remove the terror—at the "libertinism" and the "license"—of a government based on the consent of the governed.

Yet if the political significance of Shaftesbury's moral-aesthetic-sense theory was to be obscured from view in the years that followed, this occurred because Shaftesbury himself was driven from the political field. For the Greek and Roman model of a virtuous commonwealth that constantly filled his thoughts with hopes of "other Dions, other Phocions, other Catos, other Academys, another Porch" (*Life,* 83) would just as constantly fail him at the level of practical politics. Because his own brief experience as a member of Parliament would lead to a helpless sense of social corruption, Shaftesbury came to see in the new Whig order nothing more exalted than a coalition of shifting and particular interests governing the state for its own ends. Convinced that "it would have been altogether as well for my country and mankind, if I had done nothing [in Parliament], so fruitless have my endeavours been," and deeply apprehensive that "I myself grow good for nothing, but rather grow liker and liker to that sort whom I act with and converse amongst" (*Life,* 306), Shaftesbury, in the few years remaining to him, would turn from the fetid arena of contemporary politics and begin to perform the vindication of the old Whig cause—its tolerance, its disinterestedness, its liberty, its virtue—from within the genially aristocratic pages of the *Characteristics.*

Translating his political concerns into the ethical register of the *Characteristics,* Shaftesbury would then submerge even those urgent ethical preoccupations beneath the emollient artifice of his essayistic style ("A rule, viz.: Nothing in the text but what shall be of easy, smooth, and polite reading, without seeming difficulty, or hard study" [*Second Characters,* 8]).[12] Performed in the spirit of his admired Cambridge Platonists, who ever studied, in the words of Bishop Burnet, to "take men off from being in parties, or from narrow notions, from superstitious conceits and fierceness about opinions,"[13] Shaftesbury's double displacement first of the political onto the ethical and then of the ethical onto the aesthetic would effectively obscure in later years the ideological role of his writing in assisting to legitimate the Whig consensual polity.

Nonetheless, this essential role of the moral-aesthetic sense in Whig legitimation will be glimpsed whenever the claim is advanced that political liberty improves the "liberal" arts—a claim that Shaftesbury himself was among the first to make in England. "When the free spirit of a nation turns itself" to architecture, painting and sculpture, as Shaftesbury declared in a letter to the Whig patriarch Lord Somers in 1712, "judgments are formed; critics arise; the public eye and ear improve." Nothing is so improving, he continued, "so congenial to the liberal arts, as that reigning liberty and high spirit of a people, which from the habit of judging in the highest matters for themselves, makes them freely judge of other subjects, and enter thoroughly into the characters as well of men and manners, as of the products or works of men, in art and science" (*Second Characters,* 22–23).

Here the assertion that the improving taste for the arts among the English—for Purcell's music and Palladian architecture—derives in direct terms from the liberty they enjoy from the Whig polity may be seen manifesting in ideologically transfigured form the central proposition of Locke's second treatise on government ("*Who shall be judge* whether the prince or legislative act contrary to their trust? . . . To this I reply, *The People shall be judge*" [*Two Treatises,* 426–27]) coming to be expressed in the emergently aesthetic language of connoisseurship, taste, and artistic judgment. With the extraordinary success of Shaftesbury's *Characteristics* among readers of all classes during the earlier eighteenth century,[14] meanwhile, the older association between connoisseurship and exclusively aristocratic pursuits would begin to loosen. Under the aegis of the moral-aesthetic sense—especially after Shaftesbury's doctrine was vigorously developed by Francis Hutcheson into "one of the most elaborate systems of moral philosophy which we possess" (Sidgwick, 190)—it would even become possible to regard aesthetic sensibility as a universal mode of perception associated with a certain sturdy English liberty or independence of mind. Thus, for instance, John Armstrong wrote in "Taste: An Epistle to a Young Critic" (1753),

> Judge for yourself; and as you find report
> Of wit as freely as of beef or port.
> Zounds! shall a pert or bluff important wight,
> Whose brain is fanciless, whose blood is white;
> A mumbling ape of taste; prescribe us laws
> To try the poets, for no better cause
> Than that he boasts *per ann.* ten thousand clear,
> Yelps in the House, or barely sits a Peer?
> For shame! for shame! the liberal British soul
> To stoop to any stale dictator's rule!

(132)

"Judge for yourself": presented under a myriad apparently apolitical guises, this notion nurtured within the "liberal British soul," this idea of the reciprocal and mutually sustaining relationship between aesthetic and political judgment, would form the core of the emergent Whig aesthetic tradition. Although Shaftesbury himself would quietly slip first into contumely and then into oblivion as an ethical philosopher—Thomas Gray remarking in 1758 with a brusque contempt that the "interval of above forty years has pretty well destroyed the charm. A dead lord ranks but with commoners" (2:583)—the sociopolitical dimensions of Shaftesbury's thought would continue to enlarge the tradition of Germano-Hellenism developing outside of England with J. J. Winckelmann, Johann Wolfgang von Goethe, Friedrich Schiller, Friedrich Hölderlin, and G. W. F. Hegel,[15] who would discover in the third earl's moral-sense theory a means of combatting these accelerating forces of alienation and disintegration.

In Shaftesbury's writings, to be sure, the ideal to which his German successors appealed had been only intermittently glimpsed. Yet it was always there, in the notion of an "equal commonwealth" as it is itself an object of moral and aesthetic delight. "What is there in the world that has more of beauty," Shaftesbury asked, "or that gives the idea of the *to kalon* more perfect and sensible than the view of an equal commonwealth, or city, founded on good laws?" (*Life,* 44–45). For at such moments the *isonomia* or equality of political status represented in such a commonwealth becomes the object of an admiration that includes but is not limited to the aesthetic. Nonetheless, lying just beyond the discursive horizon may be glimpsed the historical transformation that will issue in the ideal so famously enunciated in Schiller's *On the Aesthetic Education of Man* (1795), the ideal of the aesthetic state where everything, "even the tool which serves—is a free citizen, having equal rights with the noblest" (219).

Shaftesbury's original note of historical and political urgency would once again be heard only when his larger claims for the moral-aesthetic sense—for its disinterestedness, its universality, its transcendental filiations with the Platonic *to kalon,* and its ethical solidarity with the Stoic *sensus communis*—had returned through the new channel of Kantian and post-Kantian aesthetic philosophy with transformative force, especially among the Victorians. Yet when that note sounded again—in Ruskin's ideal of Gothic, Morris's brotherly company of art, Arnold's vision of Hellenism as a redemptive power within Victorian culture—the possibility of a paradox never perceived as such by Shaftesbury or his eighteenth-century admirers will return to haunt the Whig aesthetic tradition.

This is the paradox that Shaftesbury, painfully aware that the age of aristocracy and divine right is at an end and trying desperately to legitimate an alternative basis of civic authority, may have unconsciously arrived at the notion of the moral-aesthetic sense as a *sensus communis* by projecting his own aristocratic sensibility outward onto humanity as a whole. The moral sense proclaimed and celebrated in the *Characteristics* would itself on this account be nothing more than the dying echo of an aristocratic ideology of chivalric honor and selflessness, a last vestige of that older world of divine right and absolutist power with which Shaftesbury had always thought himself to be engaged in antagonistic struggle.

In the eighteenth century, the solitary voice crying out that some such paradox as this lies at the heart of Shaftesbury's system belongs to Mandeville, whose own writings are driven by a contemptuous amazement that such nonsense as the idea of a universal disposition toward virtue and beauty is taken seriously in England. For it is not simply that the perpetual "hunting after this *pulchrum* and *honestum* is not much better than a wild-goose-chase" (1:331), as Mandeville impatiently puts it, but that the whole enterprise is so obviously that of a pampered nobleman who has mistaken his own sensibility—the product of a privileged and unrepeatable set of historical contingencies—for that of humankind generally: "A man that has been brought up in ease and affluence, if he is of a quiet indolent nature, learns to shun every thing that is troublesome, and . . . may in such happy circumstances have a better opinion of his inward state than it really deserves, and believe himself virtuous, because his passions lie dormant" (1:331–32).

The paradox of Shaftesbury's position as Mandeville grasps it and as it would resurface to disrupt the utopian projects of aesthetic democracy in Victorian England, is not traceable as such to its proclamation of an innate human virtue. For this would have been for Mandeville, a Hobbesian egoist whose gloomy view of human nature so often resembled that of Augustinian Christianity, simply a local instance of the larger error committed by eighteenth-century Pelagianism: the tendency, in arguing that the religious myth of original sin is only a myth, to go to the opposite extreme of imagining that human moral nature is essentially virtuous. Instead, the error lying at the center of Shaftesbury's theory is for Mandeville more specific: Shaftesbury, spared by the good fortune of his gentle birth from the evils and temptations to which ordinary men and women are continuously subject, never came to understand his own nature as a human creature. The paradox of the *Characteristics* is thus that, even as it undertakes to offer moral guidance to actual men and women, its precepts could be imagined working only in some impossible society peopled exclusively by virtuous nobles like Shaftesbury himself.

Yet the paradox posed a deeper difficulty as well. For the legitimacy of the liberal polity itself was, as we have seen, bound up at a constitutive level with ideas of art and aesthetic capacity, with disinterestedness and "judging for yourself," with liberty and "license." When, in the aftermath of the Second Reform Bill agitation, Arnold appealed to "our sense for conduct" and "our sense for beauty"—which is nothing other than Shaftesbury's moral-aesthetic sense finding new expression in a Victorian register—he deploys the positive resources of the Whig aesthetic tradition to relegitimate the Victorian liberal polity, reconnecting it through "Culture" and "Hellenism" and "ideas" to a realm of transcendental value. The relation between liberalism and the aesthetic sphere is, however, a reciprocal one and will always harbor a negative potentiality. If the liberal polity may at first hope for relegitimation through the culture and Hellenism of Arnold, it will later come to dread the possibility of its own delegitimation through the liberty and license of Wilde.

As Matthew Arnold looked beyond the unruly working-class crowd stoning windows in Chester Square, then, he confronted the deeper anarchy, affecting every class, flowing out of the central liberal principle of "Doing as One Likes." Surveying in *Culture and Anarchy* the most recent and most characteristic expressions of this "central idea of English life and politics"—of the lower class to smash park railings and house windows, of the middle class to try to marry its deceased wife's sister and of the nobility to hunt with appropriate ceremony the vermin appropriate to its rank—Arnold recognized that "the assertion of personal liberty" represented the monstrous growth of a Whig liberty that, having lost its moorings in the transcendental realm of ideas and *Geist,* now threatened England with palpable danger.

Already, in the years preceding the Hyde Park riots, Arnold had felt oppressed by the approach of national decay and supercession. "I have a conviction," he gloomily wrote to his youngest sister in 1865, "that there is a real, an almost imminent danger of England losing immeasurably in all ways, declining into a sort of greater Holland, for want of what I must still call ideas, for want of perceiving how the world is going and must go, and preparing herself accordingly" (*Letters,* 1:309–10). This foreboding had only been intensified by his recent tour of duty as a school inspector on the Continent, where he had repeatedly encountered Europeans who viewed English culture with contempt, and by his own inability to unsettle the serene complacency of his countrymen, many of whom were still psychically living off the now antique and irrelevant victory of Waterloo, by communicating to the English any real awareness of that contempt.

At the same time, Arnold's overwhelming sense of the inevitable historical forces sweeping England against its will into an unrecognizable future allowed him to see that none of the contemporary alternatives to the Victorian liberal polity could offer any hope: not the aristocratic "heroarchy" proposed by Thomas Carlyle, not the theocratic state advanced by John Henry Newman, and not the democratic state urged by John Bright. Born of nostalgia for a lost world of certitude, Carlyle's government by heroes seemed to Arnold nothing more than a pleasing if deluded fantasy of careless noble grace in a shrunken tradesmen's world. Worse, such aristocratic "Barbarians," too dim to perceive the way the world was going and must go, lay like "an *incubus*" upon the breast of the middle classes (*Letters,* 2:229), reinforcing in those classes precisely the imaginative paralysis already induced in them by their own cults of respectability and religion.

If Newman's implicitly theocratic polity seemed to promise a state where the crippling deformations and constraint of the Dissenting middle classes might be perfectly healed, there, too, Arnold's sense of a zeitgeist more powerful than Newman's personal vision told him that the world had changed beyond recall. A frank reading of the German Higher Criticism of the Bible must, Arnold thought, convince any unblinkered reader that all religion making supernatural claims was doomed and that all such political hopes based, as Newman's were, on such a foundation must inevitably fail as well.

Yet even as the last remnants of the old absolutist authority of Leviathan and the scriptural authority of patriarchy were vanishing, swept away as though by a resistless modern tide, Arnold saw that the democratic state premised on Bright's laissez-faire capitalism would only exacerbate the already crippling deficiencies so evident in the contemporary Dissenting middle classes, which largely constituted the ranks of Arnold's "Philistines" and, more to the point, which would be catapulted by the Second Reform Bill into a numerical majority within the expanded electorate (Wilson, xv). Driven by the inescapable logic of representative government, by which "every one of our governors has all possible temptation, instead of setting up before the governed who elect him, and on whose favour he depends, a high standard of right reason, to accommodate himself as much as possible to their natural taste for the bathos" (Arnold, *Culture and Anarchy,* 150), the political transformation empowering the Dissenting middle classes would entail vast cultural consequences. It would not be long, Arnold saw, before their political power would become cultural preponderance.

Cut off from membership in the House of Commons until 1828, from graduation from Oxford and Cambridge until 1854 and 1856, respectively, and from the civil service effectively until 1871, the Dissenting middle classes had been thrown back upon what Arnold was compelled to recognize as a tenacious religious tradition. During their long cultural isolation, Dissenters had created a world centered in chapel going, tea drinking, and tract reading and focused exclusively, as it seemed, on two ends, making an earthly fortune and winning a heavenly reward. It was, said Arnold, an illiberal, dismal life. The great thing, as he declared in a letter to his mother, would thus be "to drag the dissenting middle class into the great public arena of life and discussion, and not let it remain in its isolation. All its faults come from that isolation" (*Letters,* 1:368). In the formative period of the modern English polity, the third earl of Shaftesbury's absorbing fear had been that the Whig cause would be undone by a Court-directed materialism of luxury and corruption. More than 150 years later, Arnold came to fear the effects of a much more pervasive materialism: the reward system of Philistine commerce and religion with its honeyed promises of earthly riches and heavenly crowns.

The apocalyptic note heard so repeatedly in *Culture and Anarchy* arises because Arnold has perceived in the ignobility of middle-class life—the Philistine insensibility to "ideas," beauty, and *Geist*—the terrible danger, so immediately evident to a mind trained in liberal assumptions, that the English polity has utterly lost contact with any realm of transcendental value. This is why it was not simply inadequate but wholly pernicious for nineteenth-century liberals vacuously to congratulate themselves that in England every man was free to say what he liked, unless, as Arnold insisted, "what men say, when they may say what they like, is worth saying,—has good in it, and more good than bad" (*Culture and Anarchy,* 96). For this superstitious worship of the mere political apparatus of "freedom," like the no less superstitious conviction that wealth, population, or railroads could constitute England's greatness, was nothing more than a worship of machinery.

This is the moment in which Arnold, moved to his call for Hellenism, ideas, disinterestedness as if by a subconscious ideological imperative, returns to the fountain of legitimation for the liberal polity that Shaftesbury had been led to establish in the moral-aesthetic realm. Yet Arnold's return to the body of moral and aesthetic theory we now associate with Shaftesbury could not be a return directly to Shaftesbury's writings. For by the middle of the nineteenth century the third earl was largely unread and unknown, his ideas dispersed through a score of different authors, his oeuvre made synonymous with what is his least representative work, *The Moralists,* whose mode of Platonic dialogue was, as Shaftesbury himself admitted, "too ponderous and vast" (*Second Characters,* 7). Shaftesbury lived on in the nineteenth century merely as what even Leslie Stephen did not hesitate to call "a second-rate English author of Queen Anne's time" (81).

If Arnold's terms of Hellenism and disinterestedness are ultimately Shaftesburian, then, it is because his turn toward an idealized Greece draws at such moments on all that Shaftesbury had become in the intervening years, especially all that Shaftesbury's moral-aesthetic-sense theory had become among the Germans. Greece had been for Shaftesbury himself primarily a society in which a high level of artistic achievement, and, even more, the appreciation of beauty by the populace as a whole, were the natural concomitants of civic liberty. In Greece alone—"that sole polite, most civilised, and accomplished nation" (*Characteristics,* 2:241)—the freedom of ordinary citizens to participate meaningfully in the life of their community had produced unequaled artistic consequences in the perfection of Hellenic arts and letters.

In the century after Shaftesbury's death, however, with Winckelmann and the tradition of Germano-Hellenism deriving from him, Greece itself had become a primary object of aesthetic contemplation. Gazing upon a few unrepresentative copies of Hellenic sculpture, first in Dresden and then in Rome, Winckelmann had penetrated as though by a power of divination to the qualities of noble simplicity and calm grandeur in Phidian sculpture—even though genuinely Phidian statues would not be recovered and visible to students of classical antiquity for years yet. "By no people," as Winckelmann declared peremptorily in his famous *History of Ancient Art* (1764) in a passage later quoted in Pater's *Renaissance,* "has beauty been so highly esteemed as by the Greeks." At this moment of radical transmutation, an imagined Hellenic polity having itself no idea of beauty as a separate category of perception,[16] a social order in which painting, music, sculpture, poetry, and architecture had simply been features of a lived wholeness of collective existence, becomes in the fallen mid-eighteenth-century world of a diminished modernity at once a model of genuine civilization and a monitory parable.

In the *History* and in the explosive little pamphlet Winckelmann published in 1755, *Thoughts on the Imitation of Greek Works of Art in Painting and Sculpture,* we may trace at a submerged level of implication the momentous process through which the Whig political order of natural sociability that Shaftesbury had once sought to legitimate by connecting it to the realm of *to kalon* and the *sensus communis* came to be projected onto historical Greece. For Winckelmann, reading Shaftesbury, *Cato's Letters,* and Hume as a concerted act of resistance to an absolutist France tyrannizing over a fragmented and impoverished Germany would transform Hellas into nothing less than a new commonwealth of perfect art and freedom—a gleaming utopian paradigm for modern societies threatened with moral or spiritual disintegration.

The influence of Winckelmann's vision of Greek society was enormous, and within a generation his aestheticized Greece would be taken by European and English writers alike—by Goethe and Schiller, Hölderlin and Humboldt, Shelley, Hazlitt, and Keats—as corresponding to a Greece that had once actually existed in history. Among these writers it is Schiller whose preoccupation with Greece marks a last decisive transformation of the idea. Schiller's *On the Aesthetic Education of Man* (1795), attempting nothing less than to enunciate a theory of the "aesthetic state" (*der ästhetische Staat*), provides the first moment at which the aesthetic sense is presumed to possess a power of agency in the world, not simply to register beauty in a passive way but to suggest a vital means of altering social reality.

Written in the shadow of the Terror that had arisen in revolutionary

France under the banner of an abstract liberty and equality, Schiller's *Aesthetic Education* confronts at the deepest level the idea of Robespierre or revolution as the agent of history and of history as the progressive process that, harsh as its bloody dictates may be for individuals caught in any given local situation, works ultimately toward the emancipation of humankind as a whole. It is preeminently to the Terror that Schiller owes his clairvoyant sense of what in our time has come to be known, in the phrase of Max Horkheimer and Theodor Adorno, as the dialectic of enlightenment: the inevitable human price paid for material progress in the form of a blindly instrumental rationality that drains the world of moral and aesthetic value and an economic specialization that leads to individual alienation as well as the fragmentation of the social whole.

Aesthetic Education dissented early and eloquently from the uncritical worship of a historical progress achieved through the lopsided specialization of human powers: "In what kind of relation would we stand to either past or future ages if the development of human nature were to make such sacrifice necessary? We would have been the serfs of mankind; for several millennia we would have done slaves' work for them, and our mutilated nature [*unsrer verstümmelten Natur*] would bear impressed upon it the shameful marks of this servitude" (43). Here Schiller strikes a distinctively German note, as Roy Pascal has emphasized, in laying his stress upon the "quality of personal life, the etiolation of the personality, the degrading of the divine image." What Scotsmen trained in the civil society tradition of Adam Ferguson and John Millar can regard and regret with equanimity, becomes by contrast for the Germans, says Pascal, "a matter of profoundest and most immediate concern" (16). This intensely moral protest would in turn be absorbed within what Raymond Williams has analyzed as a peculiarly English "tradition of culture." Thus, Schiller's dissent would ultimately be taken up by Ruskin, Morris, and Pater, as it was by Arnold in speaking of "incomplete and mutilated men" and of the passing generations "sacrificed" (*Culture and Anarchy,* 236, 105).

Schiller's profoundly original and influential move, Fredric Jameson has said, was to have "transferred the notion of the division of labor, of economic specialization, from the social classes to the inner functioning of the mind" (87). In the midst of the psychic stunting and social fragmentation imposed by resistless forces of modernity, Schiller would derive from the vision of Greece as aesthetic state—that idealized polity first beheld by Winckelmann as he had gazed back at Greek civilization through the medium of Shaftesburian moral theory—the dynamic principle of the aesthetic *Spieltrieb* (play-drive). This transformative power mediates between the realm of reason and the realm of action and thus harmonizes the human capacities in a world increasingly given over to fragmentation or alienation.[17]

Schiller's main philosophical debt at such moments is to Kant and specifically to the move through which Kant, himself drawing on Shaftesbury's account of the moral sense as a *sensus communis,*[18] had in the "Third Critique" established aesthetic judgment as a subjectively pleasurable concert of disinterested, purposive, and free mental activity that was simultaneously universal, or true for everyone. Yet Schiller's evident shift of emphasis here is nonetheless revolutionary in its implications, for where both Shaftesbury and Kant had been content to treat the sense of beauty as an active power only within the mind, Schiller insists on perceiving in it a transformative power in the social sphere, a source of moral regeneration in a world awakening to the bleaker consequences of historical progress.

In place of those instruments of social improvement offered by the ideologues of revolutionary France, Schiller argues, there must be found "some instrument not provided by the State"—"this instrument," he concludes, "is Fine Art" (*Aesthetic Education,* 55). Through what Schiller calls aesthetic education, through what Ruskin would later call "the promulgation of art-knowledge," and what Morris would call the "democracy of the arts," the psychic harmony and social cohesion that the Greeks had once achieved through the providential gifts of nature and circumstance might be recovered and made available to European men and women living amid the disintegrative circumstances of modernity.

Schiller's notion of the sense of beauty as possessing a transformative or redemptive power thus provides the philosophical resource that would, as mediated through the writing of Carlyle and Samuel Taylor Coleridge, fuel the great transformative utopian projects of Victorian Aestheticism: the Gothic ideals urged by Ruskin and Morris, the new English Renaissance promised by Pater and Wilde. For the power or agency granted to the aesthetic sense in Schiller's theory represents a reawakening after long silence of the overtones of political urgency originating in Shaftesbury's notion of the moral-aesthetic sense as a *sensus communis* and the basis of a liberal social order. Jameson has once again made this practical and political dimension to Schiller's aesthetic theory compelling through his steady insistence that, in art, "the experience of the imaginary offers (in an imaginary mode) that total satisfaction of the personality and of Being in the light of which the real world stands condemned, in the light of which the Utopian idea, the revolutionary blueprint, may be conceived" (90).

At the same time, Schiller's *Aesthetic Education* raises a new danger to the liberal polity that would have been inconceivable to Shaftesbury, who had imagined the sense of beauty as leading both the well-bred man and the common man steadily toward the higher realm of *to kalon* where reside "the greatest realities of things, especially the beauty and order of affections." For in Schiller, the older association of beauty and morality so evident in Shaftesbury's moral-aesthetic sense or in Kant's "Third Critique" begins to loosen, and the ontological sphere of value toward which Shaftesbury constantly gestured as *to kalon* or Kant pointed as the "supersensible" (*das Uebersinnliche*) begins to recede. The danger that emerges in Schiller's *Aesthetic Education,* as Charles Taylor has said, is not simply that "beauty might offer us a higher goal" (*Sources,* 422), but that "this higher fulfillment might take us outside the received morality" (423).

This is the danger, in short, of a radically autonomous subjectivity, precisely as Courthope had sensed it in the culture of Arnold, Pater, Ruskin, Morris, and others of the modern aesthetic school. "What, in a word, is the general tendency of 'Culture,'" Courthope asked, "but to encourage a passion for private and impossible ideals?" Is not this note of "an almost sublime egotism," he continued, what we hear in *Fors Clavigera* when Ruskin complained so extravagantly, "I am left utterly stranded and alone in life and in thought" ("Modern Culture," 413)? Does not Arnold's own notable scheme of "Culture," through which selfishness is somehow to be cured by means of self, in fact require Arnold to do nothing else than "enforce a law, of which he would abolish the sanction" (399)?

As Courthope elaborated his view of Arnold, Ruskin, and Pater as partisans of "liberalism, or religion based on self-worship, of which self culture is the last and the logical development" (412), he unerringly pointed to the ideological blind spots and evasions that Victorian liberalism, in its recent exertions on behalf of the Second Reform Bill, had exposed to view. Did Arnold deplore the lack in England of any "paramount authority," any notion of the centralized state? All very true, Courthope conceded, but the criticism "comes rather strangely from one of a party whose whole policy has been to *remove* power from the aristocracy, which, however imperfect, was certainly a centre, and to vest it exclusively in the middle class, which, outside the Constitution, has neither unity nor cohesion" (400; emphasis added). Did Pater and J. A. Symonds idolize ancient Greece? It is a striking comment on our modern English Renaissance, Courthope noted, "that at the very moment when Hellenism is being held up before us as the mirror of perfection, the University of Oxford has taken the first step towards discouraging the study of Greek" ("Renaissance," 30).

Writing in the midst of intensely specific and partisan conflicts—the Tory victory in the general election of 1873, the battle over the Oxford Professorship of Poetry in 1877—Courthope came to explore with an instinctive political touch the contradictions and omissions that had been written into the Whig aesthetic tradition long before, when liberalism had undertaken to found an authoritative polity upon a nonauthoritarian basis. Protesting "a school of artists, poets, and critics, who live in an atmosphere of exquisite superiority" ("Progress," 50) and desiring a culture "that shall be breathed from the common air, not elaborated out of the individual mind" ("Modern Culture," 414), Courthope brought partially into view the repressed paradox within aesthetic liberalism—of an aristocratic gift projected as a democratic endowment that Mandeville had discovered so many years before.

Yet the more daunting adversary for the writers of Victorian Aestheticism—daunting because so continually disruptive of their work and thought—would always be less a given, named antagonist such as Courthope than the continually repressed suspicion that Mandeville had been right after all. Aestheticist writers feared that the generality of humankind were mere creatures of appetite and unreason, capable of caring about nothing higher, as Carlyle said in "Shooting Niagara," than "the appetites of their own huge belly, and the readiest method of assuaging these" (315–16). The bleak and unbearable possibility that haunted Aestheticism throughout the later nineteenth century is that Shaftesbury's vision of the liberal polity—of equal commonwealths and disinterestedness, of the *sensus communis* and "judging for yourself"—had been no more, in the longer run, than an insubstantial dream, the reverie of a nobleman determined to discover in humankind as a whole a capacity to appreciate moral beauty given in every age only to a few. The manner in which each of the major writers in its tradition came to grips with this repressed possibility gave Aestheticism its underlying continuity and dynamism as a major movement in Victorian culture.

II

Ruskin's Law in Art

Now observe—I am not engaged in selfish cultivation of critical acumen, but in ardent endeavour to spread the love and knowledge of art among all classes;—and secondly, that the love and knowledge I would communicate are not of technicalities and fancies of men, but of the universal system of nature—as interpreted and rendered stable by art.

(Ruskin, Letter to Osborne Gordon)

FOR VICTORIANS at midcentury the belief that art could transform society had a name, and that name was John Ruskin. The most compelling vision of art as the incarnation of an ideal polity was the picture of Gothic architecture Ruskin gave in "The Nature of Gothic," the chapter from *The Stones of Venice* that constitutes his most famous single piece of writing. Ruskin's depiction of the order of life implied by Gothic architecture, a life irradiated by the joy of cooperative, meaningful work within and for an organic social whole, brought about not simply a transformation in the Victorian built environment but an inward renovation among those who became, in whatever degree or way, his followers.

Two years after Ruskin's death in 1900, Frederic Harrison praised him as the man "who in the English-speaking world left the most direct and most visible imprint of his tastes and thoughts" (*John Ruskin,* 1). For by 1902 Ruskin's influence had indeed taken shape throughout the parishes of England and America, his call for a new architecture having assumed palpable form in countless neo-Gothic churches, museums, and other public buildings as well as in domestic architecture. If the Victorian Gothic revival owed as much to Sir Walter Scott, A. W. N. Pugin and the Camden Society as to Ruskin, he nonetheless freed the movement from its antiquarianism and ecclesiasticism to make it the vehicle for profound human hopes of social renewal. Turning his enthusiasm and energy to the new Oxford Museum of Natural History (1855–60), for instance, Ruskin inflected the architects' Gothic design with new decorative elements of color and individualized carving: the museum's capitals, richly incised with plant and animal forms (no two alike), would satisfy both the middle-class visitor's desire for beauty and knowledge and the working-class artisan's need for beauty and self-expression, while the museum itself would serve the nation's requirements in science and health.[1]

Yet beyond any influence that Ruskin achieved as an architectural writer or as a lecturer and drawing master in venues ranging from the Working Men's College in London to the Sheldonian Theatre in Oxford, his power of speaking from the printed page to each individual reader as an individual constituted the core of his extraordinary influence. Whatever the snobbish idolatries of the later Ruskin Societies, whatever the deluded ambitions of a Guild of St. George or a Ruskin, Tennessee, Ruskin's inspirational, transformative power upon two generations of Victorians became his enduring legacy. In the words of one of his followers, Ruskin "smashed up for ever the narrow technicalities of artists, and altered the point of view not only for them, but for the whole world, and gave the seeing eye, and thought, and feeling a practical reality which they will never lose but never had before" (Ruskin, *Works,* 5: lxi). In the words of another disciple, "Ah, my Ruskin, it is you who give heart to the faint-hearted, who purify the air, who make it possible for us to cry, and to believe, *Work, good work, and for nothing!*" (Cobden-Sanderson, 1:302).

Ruskin's enormous influence on Victorians arose from the unique conjunction of two ongoing processes: in the early 1850s his audiences became uniquely ready to hear what he during this same period became uniquely able to say. By 1851, the year of both the first volume of *Stones of Venice* and of the great Crystal Palace exhibition in London, Ruskin's middle-class readers had entered a period of expansive economic growth and, after the Chartist agitations and famine-driven Irish immigration of the 1840s, of relative domestic tranquillity. This was the time of the "Victorian noon," in Carl Dawson's phrase, when the almost grotesque abundance poured out in the more than 100,000 Crystal Palace exhibits—reapers, diamonds, stuffed frogs, the electric telegraph, the statue of Queen Victoria rendered in zinc—would come to symbolize the vast mid-Victorian economic plenitude.[2] To the now prospering but culturally intimidated middle classes that were ready, as David DeLaura has argued, to venture into this new sensate and acquisitive culture, provided that they would not lose the advantages of the older religious culture (380), Ruskin would become the single indispensable guide.

With the publication of the second volume of *Stones of Venice* in 1853, there appeared in "The Nature of Gothic" the answerable gospel for this middle-class progressivism: that "liberal tract," as James Sherburne has called it (53), that "necessary and inevitable" utterance, as William Morris considered it ("Preface," i), that "creed of Liberalism in its most noble and generous form," as even W. J. Courthope would declare it to be ("Progress," 73). Ruskin's quenchless eloquence made the aesthetic dimension of society and the social dimension of art cohere as never before into a single, vitally important sphere. In precisely the same way, his energy and fanatical reverence for art charged that sphere, as Paul Sawyer has argued in a recent study, with "the force to revolutionize nineteenth-century society" (103). In its dependence on the myth of the Fall, with its picture of the primacy of innocence and the externality of sin, Ruskin's account of Venice represented nothing less than a simultaneous acceptance and rejection of human sinfulness, offering the individual Victorian "hope for the survival of the original, pure energy of childhood through accidents and losses" while offering the Victorian age "the survival of great art as a propulsive force for collective renewal" (Sawyer, 103).

If Ruskin's "Nature of Gothic" caught his middle-class readers in the moment of their expanding cultural power and social hope, the work represented a similarly opportune moment in Ruskin's own career. For the work was written when his religious faith remained firm enough to endow his assumptions about beauty and art with a metaphysical basis yet supple enough to allow the assumptions of the Whig aesthetic tradition an unconstricted voice—the voice that would catch the ear of his Anglo-American audiences. This window of aesthetic liberalism in Ruskin's career opened after he had broken free from the intense religious and aesthetic parochialism of his Evangelical home and before the effects of his failures in faith, love, and work would move him to reinvoke the structures of patriarchal control in a desperate attempt to master what he experienced as a widening anarchy both inside and outside himself.

Newly attentive to politics in the disturbing aftermath of that year of revolutions, 1848, yet buoyed by confidence and mental calm, his art expertise widening and maturing after repeated tours of Italy, yet his religious faith still relatively unperplexed, Ruskin was intensely moved by the decaying architectural fabric of Venice as the legible aesthetic face of its moral and political legitimacy. During this period, Ruskin achieved a moment of equipoise in which the voices of Shaftesbury and the Common Sense philosophers he had bred in Scotland could join with Aristotle, Bishop Butler, and others of the Oxford *Literae humaniores* curriculum and speak unhindered about the identity of the moral and the aesthetic and about the human mind in its disinterestedness and pleasurable energy of contemplation.[3]

In this way, the force of Ruskin's religious convictions for a brief period organized and imparted energy to ideas that belonged to a parallel universe of thought—the tradition of Whig aesthetics. Once Ruskin's religious faith broke up in the long process of transformation for which his "unconversion" of 1858 in Turin became the central symbol, the ideas of liberty, universal aesthetic capacity, individuality, and all the other ostensibly liberal sympathies within his idea of Gothic collapsed for lack of an authenticating ground. Ruskin set them aside for patriarchal and utilitarian principles that seemed to him more authoritative because he knew them to be reliably rooted in the ancient and self-evident verities of order and use. But until he was driven to this position in the later 1860s and 1870s under the relentless pressures of his failed work, his disappointed love, and his mental disorder, which were to culminate in the disastrous Whistler lawsuit in 1877–78, Ruskin's message—the ideal of Gothic that was to serve as a manifesto for aesthetic democracy from the days of the Working Men's College to those of Frank Lloyd Wright—seemed to his legion of readers to confer upon the serenely confident, forward-flowing currents of liberalism the blessings of religious orthodoxy and Romantic idealism. In short, Ruskin's message succeeded with so many Victorians because Ruskin, that "violent Illiberal," that Tory of the old school, as he liked to call himself, seemed for a brief but persuasive period so much like a Whig.[4]

Ruskin's early Evangelical faith provided the sustaining medium for beliefs about the freedom and moral equality of persons, human nature in its fullest individuality, and the pleasurableness and disinterestedness of aesthetic contemplation that Ruskin silently absorbed from the Whig aesthetic tradition flowing from Shaftesbury. The residual power imparted to the aesthetic liberalism of "The Nature of Gothic" may be seen in its fullest potency in Ruskin's early defense of J. M. W. Turner in *Modern Painters.* Devoted to showing Victorians in exhaustive yet exhilarating detail why Turner, as Ruskin declared, was "the greatest painter of *all* time; a man with whose supremacy of power no intellect of past ages can be put in comparison for a moment" (*Works,* 3:617), the first two volumes of Ruskin's *Modern Painters* (1843, 1846) undertook to show that Turner was supreme among artists because his landscapes were so superlatively true to the "facts" of the natural world.

The great virtue of this line of defense was that it allowed Ruskin to attach Turner's art to religious truth in an easy, unproblematic chain. For if Turner's canvases were true to nature, and "the truth of nature is a part of the truth of God" (3:141), then Turner's art was ultimately grounded in the firm truth of the Protestant religion, and God was thus the final guarantor of value in Turner's art—its axiological anchor. As he launches his defense of Turner, Ruskin's aesthetic theory is, as George Landow has argued in extensive detail, theocentric. Within this aesthetic Ruskin's mimetic and teleological assumptions in particular would supply a vital energy to the specifically liberal impulse within *Stones of Venice.*

This is so because Ruskin's mimetic assumption made all questions of quality, value, or "standards" in art seem relatively simple and hence accessible to his aesthetically uninitiated audience. Unlike the bewildering mysteries of connoisseurship or the alarming contentions of "taste," Ruskin's mimetic criterion of "truth" and the "facts of representation" could be corroborated by virtually anyone who had seen the original "fact" in nature. The perplexities of aesthetically inexperienced readers would vanish before "the certain test of goodness and badness"—that is, before the calm question, "Is it so? Is that the way a stone is shaped, the way a cloud is wreathed, the way a leaf is veined?" (5:180). Thus, even a miserable slum dweller could be a potential expert on the sky.

In this context, Ruskin's own independent position relative to the established cultural authorities may be seen to recapitulate that of the artist he so passionately championed. For Turner, as Ruskin fiercely declared, "is a man of inferior birth and no education," "whose brow is hard with the spray of a hundred storms" (*Works,* 3:673, 647). Ruskin's defiant posture toward the Old Master tradition and the vacuous dilettantes who served as its custodians during the 1830s and 1840s proved bracing to his culturally aspirant but inexperienced readers, rallying to his side those upstart classes and countries who felt a quickened allegiance to the new (see Landow, "There Began to Be a Great Talking").

Ruskin's mimetic theory of art allowed him also to pass along to his readers a sense of cultural competence and even something of his own authoritativeness. For the eternal truth of Christianity mediated through nature and in turn transmitted through Turner's art assured his audience that by attending to art seriously they were engaging with a realm governed by principles of immutable religious law rather than by the confusing and fallible dicta of mere human opinion. To his readers among the Dissenting sects, immured in their long isolation from national life, Ruskin's invocation of "law" held out an additional promise: that the English cultural establishment would become genuinely open to them, governed as it must be by art principles both pious and public.

So buoyant was Ruskin's early and unproblematic faith in the "law" of religious mimeticism that it impelled him to declare to a friend in 1844 that "religion must be, and always has been, the ground and moving spirit of all great art" (*Works,* 3:670). The residual force of this same mimeticism drove Ruskin's belief that there "*was* a law in this matter: that good architecture might be indisputably discerned and divided from the bad; that the opposition in their very nature and essence was clearly visible; and that we were all of us just as unwise in disputing about the matter without reference to principle, as we should be for debating about the genuineness of a coin without ringing it" (*Stones of Venice,* 9:56).

In the same way, Ruskin's early religious belief in the providential purpose or teleology within the response to beauty gave vital support to the later liberal impulse of his work. For his early conviction that God had lovingly fitted the visible world to delight the eyes of men and women helped slowly to dissolve away the inveterate Calvinist prejudice against the physical senses among many of his readers. Ruskin himself experienced recurrent spasms of uneasiness about the place and worth of sensation in aesthetic judgment, for he knew his own experience of art and nature to be enchantingly and imperiously sensuous.[5] He was, in John D. Rosenberg's compelling description, "eye-driven, even photo-erotic, and confessed to 'a sensual faculty of pleasure in sight' to which he knew no parallel. All the forms of the visible world leaped into animate life before his eyes" (4).

Yet Ruskin recognized that to deny or discount this most puissant reality of his life would be to declare himself an orphan and outcast in the visible world. Thus, in the beginning, his defense of Turner's art drew deeply upon a powerfully religious conviction that the pleasures of the eye were mysterious but providentially bestowed gifts, never to be confused "with the blind and temporary instincts of the blood" (*Works,* 4:142n). They were instead "ultimate instincts and principles of human nature, for which no farther reason can be given than the simple will of the Deity that we should be so created" (3:109)—in short, dedicated pleasures that prompted "not only a feeling of strong affection towards the object in which they exist, but a perception of purpose and adaptation of it to our desires; a perception, therefore, of the immediate operation of the Intelligence which so formed us, and so feeds us" (4:47).

So long as Ruskin's religious faith purified the inlets of sense, the deeply sensuous experience that he knew whenever he used his eyes and his empirical understanding of beauty absorbed from Burke, Shaftesbury, and Locke were saved from the otherwise constant threat that haunted him: mere animal sensuality. In the same way, just as Ruskin's teleological premise raised the "mere sensual pleasure of the eye" (3:91) to the plane of contemplative intellect, so in turn did his teleological piety redeem beauty from all notions of mere utility or convention. From time to time, an Aristotelian hierarchy of mind over body and contemplation over physical labor would silently mold Ruskin's assumptions, encouraging him to contemn the visceral responses of the body in favor of the "higher" faculties of mind and "some sort of energy of Contemplation" or to spurn the arena of utility and habit in favor of vistas of ennobled uselessness, unmarked by any "taint" of "subserviency to life."[6]

Yet Ruskin's religious faith during this period constantly operated to remove the sting of any distinctions he might make between higher and lower, subservient and free, because his biblically toned prose seemed to translate the social discriminations of taste into the common code of universal Christian aspiration. To art-world insiders like Lady Eastlake, the peculiar language of *Modern Painters,* the "jargon of 'love,' 'wisdom,' 'fear and gladness'" that Ruskin had absorbed from Burke, together with the patois of "firm words, true message, unstinted fulness and unfailing faith" drawn from the Evangelical religious tradition, did nothing more than pad out with vulgar bombast what artists had been saying for centuries about art (432). To ordinary spectators, however—to the young, the uninitiated, and the uncertain—Ruskin's Bible-infused language, his generous gospel of the allowable pleasure and ennobling uselessness of art, and his bold revolt against the arbiters of taste came as a liberation. Here, the young men of Oxford and the young women of London said to themselves, was "a Luther of the arts," a voice "claiming for all the right of individual reading and understanding" (Hilton, 232, 227).

As Elizabeth K. Helsinger reminds us, it is easy to overestimate the democratizing thrust of Ruskin's art writing. For Ruskin will ultimately maintain what she has called "a hierarchy of vision based both on imaginative ability and on social class" (128). Thus, even when Ruskin's religious faith allowed him to be broadly generous and optimistic about human powers and potentialities, as in the first volumes of *Modern Painters,* he was likely to emphasize that high art demanded high capacities and could "only be met and understood by persons having some sort of sympathy with the high and solitary minds which produced it—sympathy only to be felt by minds in some degree high and solitary themselves" (*Works,* 3:136).

Yet even as Ruskin established these hierarchies, they assumed a dynamic function in the practical sphere where his works were being read. Richard Stein grasped this essential point when he said of this hierarchical structure that "invariably the scale becomes a ladder; the analytic distinctions between greater and lesser intellects become stages of progress in a graduated lesson in self-culture" (61). If Ruskin's theocentric mimeticism and providentialism first raised the ladder to lead his readers to God, the ladder would remain behind, after Ruskin's religious faith had failed, to become an engine of secular self-improvement and aesthetic democracy.

This larger social truth is contained within Graham Hough's Jungian argument that Ruskin in his day was "trying to bring about a psychological revolution" (12). For by vindicating the rights of the senses on behalf of a generation "by whom the sense of sight was left uncultivated as it had probably never been before" (9), Ruskin liberated visual capacities that had once been wholly subordinated to utility and convention, leading them out into a realm of open social possibilities. Helsinger's patient technical analysis of Ruskin's notion of "excursive sight" has allowed us to see more fully this realm of socially transformative potentiality. Discussing Ruskin's purging and empowering of the visual sense in terms of a "democritization of imaginative perception," Helsinger demonstrates that Ruskin "democratizes" visual perception by shifting the model of aesthetic experience from the solitary and heroic partaker of the sublime to the more sociable tourists of the picturesque. As a result, his new emphasis on active or "excursive" seeing and his insistence that such seeing is always a learned activity not a mysteriously bestowed gift will entail radical new sociocultural consequences (206).

The great power and influence of Ruskin's earlier art writing, then, derives from his extraordinary ability to reach beneath the understandable loyalties and insecurities of his culturally inexperienced readers and to hail them at a more fundamental level. For it was Ruskin's gift, as it was Carlyle's, "not [to] address the sense of justice or cause, but rather [to play] upon what we really value more: our imaginative view of ourselves as endowed souls." Ruskin became a great social prophet precisely because he addressed "not the outer but the inner life and populated it with images, set moving the confused spirit of possibility" (Pritchett, 490).

Here the liberal hope for aesthetic democracy takes its firmest root, not in any overt requirement of sameness or equality among people but in the universally bestowed recognition of each person's rich and indelible individuality. Upon this broad basis Ruskin raised the brief but reverberating liberalism of his middle years. This is why in *Stones of Venice* Ruskin directly solicits the attention of the ordinary, "the least learned" and "most desultory readers" (*Works,* 9:9) and proposes that such readers should determine their own course as readers: "I shall endeavour so to lead the reader forward from the foundation upwards, as that he may find out for himself the best way of doing everything. . . . I shall use no influence with him whatever, except to counteract previous prejudices, and leave him, as far as may be, free" (9:73).

This initial and essentially rhetorical device was not brushed aside by Ruskin's habitually imperious authorial gestures. Ruskin's understanding of Gothic architecture itself reinforced the focus on the idiosyncratic, imperfect, and individual qualities that he had already saluted in his audience and continued to acknowledge so eloquently throughout the three volumes of *Stones of Venice.*[7] Ruskin's focus on the individual detail and particular instance was implicitly democratic, as Richard Stein has noted, because it came implicitly from below. In Ruskin's romantic and individualistic aesthetic, "It is almost assumed that in architecture the whole is determined by the parts, as if buildings could somehow take shape spontaneously" (96). For this reason in turn, when Ruskin comes to describe the basilica of St. Mark's, the infinitely various carved capitals displace in his account any mention of the general floor plan and the architect disappears while the artisans remain.

This focus was augmented by the extraordinary endowment of life Ruskin imparted not simply to the unknown Gothic stonecutters but to the very stones themselves. Ruskin's Gothic architecture is ever animate and alive: "It can shrink into a turret, expand into a hall, coil into a staircase, or spring into a spire, with undegraded grace and unexhausted energy" (*Works,* 10:212). It is flexible and responsive: if Gothic builders "wanted a window, they opened one; a room, they added one; a buttress, they built one; utterly regardless of any established conventionalities of external appearance" (10:212). Most of all, Ruskin's restlessly fretted Gothic architecture mirrors back the emergent optimism and individualism of his middle-class audience, conscious of its imperfections yet confident of its power finally to prevail over the finished aristocratic orders. A barely suppressed class antagonism may thus be glimpsed throughout his account of the stylistic conflict between Venetian Gothic and Renaissance building—the latter refusing "the materials at the poor man's hand; it would not roof itself with thatch or shingle and black oak beams"; instead, poor people's cottages and streets "were to be thrust out of its way, as of a lower species" (11:75).

The anthropomorphized architectural fabric of Gothic, by contrast, possessed "that restlessness of the dreaming mind, that wanders hither and thither among the niches, and flickers feverishly around the pinnacles, and frets and fades in labyrinthine knots and shadows along wall and roof, and yet is not satisfied, nor shall be satisfied" (10:214). It thus expressed the enduring value and eloquent contribution of the lowest and most inarticulate elements, human and material. Each stone, as Paul Sawyer has observed, "bears the mark of a particular human testimony and therefore preserves a human life" (111), thus incarnating in historical and aesthetic terms the biblical conviction that the stone that the builders rejected could yet become the cornerstone of the Temple.

Ruskin's Gothic cathedral, then, became the material representation of an order that was doubly ideal: a supreme aesthetic artifact that was a perfect social concretion, the exquisite carapace molded by a social reality in which the freedoms and failures of average people were transfigured into the shared pleasure and dignity of all. It was "the principal admirableness of the Gothic schools of architecture, that they thus receive the results of the labour of inferior minds; and out of fragments full of imperfection, and betraying that imperfection in every touch, indulgently raise up a stately and unaccusable whole" (*Works,* 10:190).

As Ruskin's "Nature of Gothic" held out this optimistic picture of the Gothic ideal, it marked the farthest reach of his liberal sympathy, sustaining the relationship between individual action and social organism in a momentary and fragile equilibrium. For here Ruskin's liberal critique of the practice of government was matched by his equally liberal faith in the efficacy of individual action. His excoriating critique of laissez-faire economy and administration came armed, as James Sherburne has said, with an essentially voluntarist or libertarian weapon: the freedom of the consumer to choose and to boycott. Ruskin stressed this individual freedom to choose and through right choosing to effect happiness and expressed tenderness toward the hopeful, redoubled, and still only half-successful efforts of ordinary Gothic workers. These qualities combined with his electrifying condemnation of the modern industrial conditions crushing Victorian workers—"to smother their souls within them, to blight and hew into rotting pollards the suckling branches of their human intelligence, to make the flesh and skin which after the worm's work on it, is to see God, into leathern thongs to yoke machinery with" (10:192)—to bend Ruskin's words into the orbit of Victorian liberal aspirations.

Ruskin's picture of the Gothic worker and his world—an ideal world where paternalist bonds were indistinguishable from unfettered inclinations, where eager incapacity was repaid with personal joy and communal acceptance—was and remains richly persuasive, not least because it remains incomplete, unexplained, and largely implicit. It derived its energy and optimism from the residual power of Ruskin's Evangelical faith, with its devoted and deeply hopeful cherishing of imperfection as the providential sign of a final enfranchisement from all fault. It mattered little to Ruskin's readers that the means by which individual energy could be subordinated to the social whole was left largely vague or that the portrayal of the social order Ruskin saw concretized in Gothic architecture was, as John Unrau and others have since explained, largely false.[8]

Instead, the glamor of Ruskin's prose and the brilliance of his vision swept up two generations on both sides of the Atlantic and set moving in them the "spirit of possibility" so that such readers as Charles Eliot Norton would thereafter see in Gothic cathedrals "the prevalence of the democratic element in society" (*Notes of Travel,* 105) and call for an American neo-Gothic architecture that would arouse in each viewer "not merely poetic emotion, but his sympathy with the spirit and generous habits of his distant predecessors" ("Harvard," 38). Only with the annihilation of all Victorian idealisms in the mud and mustard gas of World War I would Ruskin become the impotent "Pope of Art," whose message had collapsed into what Geoffrey Grigson would so fiercely damn as "the Victorian lie" (223).

Ruskin's ideal of Gothic succeeded because the model and concrete manifestation of that ideal—the Gothic cathedral—hid its constitutive faults and confusions within. That ideal depended upon Ruskin's interpretation of Gothic as great architecture without an architect—arising with the effortless, ineffable grandeur of Alfred Tennyson's Camelot, "built / To music, therefore never built at all," as the multiplicity and independence of its parts resistlessly brought about the unity and subordination of the whole. At the same time, Ruskin's ideal drew at a deeper level upon the Christian belief in the Church as the incorporation of Christ and believers. "By sinking his moral argument in architectural description, Ruskin mediates between a particular building and an invisible idea, adumbrating at once the values of Protestantism and the power of a religious community to enfold and uplift its communicants" (Sawyer, 115).

Through the medium of his incomparable prose, Ruskin's Gothic cathedral thus came to represent in the eyes of his Victorian readers the promise of a sociality lived completely free from the competitive individualism and degrading power of markets, just as the Gothic workers themselves lived before the capitalist order enforced its maiming divisions of labor on men and women. In the name of a radical Christian ethics, Ruskin gave a Gothic habitation to the profound moral optimism and belief in sociability and ordinary people's "common sense" characteristic of the Scottish Enlightenment—the distinctive beliefs he had absorbed from his Scottish parents, from Carlyle and from reading Adam Smith, Adam Ferguson, Thomas Reid, and the other Scottish heirs of Shaftesbury.[9]

At the same time, however, Ruskin's Gothic cathedral—alive with its expressive gargoyles, its idiosyncratic capitals, its pragmatic buttresses, its unconventional windows—continued to reassure his middle-class readers that the transformative Gothic ideal was yet compatible at some level with market capitalism, so clearly did it seem to incorporate and foster the individuality, freedom, and richly various development of the ordinary citizen. These ideas were not indigenous to the Gothic past but instead extruded out of the Germano-Hellenic tradition and the premises of British middle-class liberalism.

Ruskin's Gothic ideal thus cohered and convinced because his audience responded more deeply to Ruskin's own hopefulness and moral optimism in creating it than they did to their own doubts that it might be untrue. Yet Ruskin's Gothic ideal lived for his readers preeminently through its current of electric emotion, and without the energizing pulse of a residually religious, residually hopeful emotion, his ideal might in time threaten to break apart into the heterogeneous and irreconcilable elements—Aristotelian, associationalist, intuitionist—out of which he had fused it. For this reason, even in the brief moment of Ruskin's liberalism, in his fullest sympathy toward human imperfection and the yearning after expressive freedom and happiness, were felt the first slight tremors of withdrawal: the religious faith that had supplied the transcendental ground for Ruskin's trust in the pleasure and purposelessness of art began to weaken, leaving Ruskin himself separated not simply from the unproblematic religious belief of his childhood but also from the Victorian audiences to which he had appealed through that belief. Soon he would confront them across a gulf he could neither bridge nor hide.

As Ruskin scholarship in recent years has taught us to understand, the recession of Ruskin's religious faith was neither as simple in its outline nor as decisive in its effects as Ruskin's own dramatic story of his "unconversion" at Turin in 1858 has long tended to suggest. Instead, it has become clear that Ruskin's religious doubts surfaced early, became mixed with socioeconomic and political fears, and were partially soothed but never entirely silenced by his return to a species of religious faith in the 1870s. The significance of this famous unconversion narrative thus lies less in its correspondence to actual fact than in its coherence as a symbol within Ruskin's own self-understanding. In the same way, the importance of Ruskin's religious unconversion for any account of Victorian Aestheticism lies in the way that his experience of the sharp ebb and intermittent return of religious belief repeats on the level of an individual life the transcendental aspirations and empirical doubts continually contending within the Whig aesthetic tradition.

As long as Ruskin's religious faith seemingly continued to counteract his doubts with a current of hopeful emotion, the moral-aesthetic tradition of Shaftesbury seemed like no alien language but a cognate mode of speech—Ruskin's Evangelical God continuously supplying him with the transcendental ground that Shaftesbury had earlier located in *to kalon* and Kant had found in the "super-sensible." With God as the axiological anchor, in turn, Ruskin could tolerate such Whig ideas as the value of sensuous pleasure for human development, the possession of aesthetic judgment among all perceivers, and the importance of disinterested or nonutilitarian art. The sensualism and selfishness that Ruskin otherwise dreaded in these ideas were continuously purified by their incorporation in God's infinitely loving plan for his creatures.

Without such a God or such a plan, however, sensuous joy and disinterested art seemed to float dangerously free into a realm he identified with egoism and animal indulgence, while the previously celebrated and certain instincts of the heart and eye as well as the forgivable, triumphant failures of the human hand seemed to him to merge into the clamorous realm of "equality" and "liberty"—that modern chaos where the incapacity of the weak and foolish sought to tyrannize over the natural sovereignty of the strong and wise. Thus, he came to think that his Evangelical faith had, in a complex process of duplication and substitution, invisibly sustained some of the central assumptions of Whig aesthetics in his writing. When that faith failed, the petrified simulacra it left behind—natural taste, disinterested art, allowable joy—seemed suddenly to become grotesque and intolerable fragments from a pagan anarchy. To escape them he withdrew into a utilitarian aesthetics and a Platonic Toryism, as Jeffrey Spear has termed it (3), and it was to remain for his younger disciples—Morris, Pater, and Wilde—to reassert the claims of aesthetic democracy within the Victorian liberal polity.

Within the symbolic chronology of Ruskin's own self-understanding, then, some twenty years passed between his unconversion at Turin and the public catastrophe of Whistler's 1877–78 libel suit against him. This span of time serves as the symbolic background against which Ruskin's continually shifting attitudes toward art and its vulgarization would seem to his increasingly disaffected audiences to trace a pattern of loss of faith in art as such. For by 1858, Ruskin's knowledge of art—at the outset of his career so parochially limited—had widened to include studies of the human figure as well as landscapes, the overwhelming, pagan riches of the Italian Renaissance as well as the reliably religious pre-Raphaelite Italian painters. This expanded fund of pictorial experience slowly revealed to him the inadequacy of his own earlier complacent equations between good painting and good men, between self-suppression and artistic excellence.

With this widened knowledge and sympathy, in turn, had come a corresponding contraction of certainty about art. Ruskin now felt the solvent effects of historicism and subjectivity that had previously left him untouched in his generation: "I have striven so earnestly to realize belief which I supposed to be false, and sentiment which was foreign to my temper that at last I scarcely know how far I think with other people's minds, and see with any one's eyes but my own" (*Works,* 22:10). This statement reflects the aesthetic equivalent of the change that was simultaneously taking place in Ruskin's idea of nature: once beautiful and providentially ordered, the natural world would gradually become irretrievably darkened to him—sometimes by demonic powers and at other times by the mad defacement of men, armed with geologists' hammers and driven by the unquenchable appetite for steam power.

The law Ruskin had once found in history, felt in nature, and seen in art had seemingly evaporated, leaving him with a sense of "calamitous mystery" that, even more strangely, somehow was less and less thought of as a calamity by the younger generation. "What puzzles me," he told a young woman during this time, "is how you all take things so quietly—and rest content in doubt, and perpetual questioning—with no answer" (*Correspondence,* 214). In the vacuum left by his receding faith, by his unsuccessful suit for the hand of Rose La Touche, and by his long impotence as a social reformer, Ruskin, increasingly subject to the obtrusions of mental disease, swung helplessly between amazed uncertainty and ferocious conviction. In the first mood he seemed to that acute judge of men, Benjamin Jowett, "the gentlest and most innocent of mankind, of great genius but inconsecutive" (2:257), and in the second mood he lashed out as Whistler's intemperate antagonist with all the "blind rhodomontade of reasoning and a reckless virulence of language" that Lady Eastlake had deplored in him years before (387).

This is why the aristocratic or hierarchical sympathies, which from the first had contested Ruskin's liberal impulses, now began to resurface with the recession of his religious faith. As long as Ruskin's Evangelical faith remained intact, the Protestant notion of the autonomous relationship of individual Christian to an unmediated God supplied an implicit model for other relationships—that of the beholder to the natural world, for example, or that of the citizen to the state. But the distancing or disappearance of God from this schema radically destabilized the relationship of individual to totality. Now the teleological presumption that had always guaranteed for Ruskin the worth of the individual's energy, sensuousness, and independence was melting away as well, and Ruskin could not trust such ungrounded human energies to their own free play. Where in the past the infinite distance between God and his human creatures effaced the infinitesimal differences among people, these differences now reappeared to Ruskin with new vividness and importance, so that he felt the need for a controlling hierarchy or structure to contain the unconsecrated forces of human assertion.

As Ruskin returned in imagination to the stable and comprehensible patriarchal structures of his childhood home at Herne Hill, his thinking reverted to the utilitarian and authoritarian principles that had been present in his mind from the first. Compounded of an aggressive hostility to the principles of liberty and equality together with a tolerance of fraternity only insofar as that Jacobinical principle would concede the "fact" of paternity or patriarchy (not very far at all),[10] his "violent" Toryism had lived all along beside his hopes for aesthetic education and his belief in human development in its richest diversity.

Long intent on questions of artistic rather than social justice—of doing justice to Turner before vouchsafing it to anonymous, discontented, potentially revolutionary Victorian workers—Ruskin had allowed his political Toryism to be countered and offset by his aesthetic liberalism, his faith in the universality and social value of beauty and art. Only as long as the spiritual and moral equality assumed within Christian faith sustained the Whig belief that the moral-aesthetic sense was the same in all people, high and low, learned and unlearned, could Ruskin's fear of artistic liberty and aesthetic equality continue to sleep. Now, however, with the ebbing of his hopefulness and his religious faith, with his deepening mental anguish and rising anger, precisely those Whig aesthetic principles lay exposed, deflated of their borrowed transcendental pneuma, and Ruskin began actively to spurn them.

This is why in the fifth volume of *Modern Painters* (1860), for instance, Ruskin revised the generous, Shaftesburian account of aesthetic judgment he had given in the first volume. There, filled with Shaftesbury's conviction that even "the vulgar man can feel, recognise" and that "the eye has sense of its own," Ruskin had declared that "the sensation of beauty is intuitive and necessary." He had sonorously reaffirmed this view in volume 1 of *Stones of Venice:* "I would have the reader discern [the universal and divine canons of loveliness] so quickly that, as he passes along a street, he may, by a glance of the eye, distinguish the noble from the ignoble work. He can do this, if he permit free play to his natural instincts; and all that I have to do for him is to remove from those instincts the artificial restraints which prevent their action, and to encourage them to an unaffected and unbiassed choice between right and wrong" (*Works,* 9:62). In volume 5, however, Ruskin doubted after all "the real use to mankind of . . . art; incomprehensible as it must always be to the mass of men" (*Works,* 7:441). He retracted the earlier effort to share with his readers his own gift of the "eye-glance"—that sudden and sovereign evidence of aesthetic mastery—and denied the central principle of aesthetic democracy, the universality of aesthetic taste: "True taste, or the instantaneous preference of the noble thing to the ignoble . . . so far as it depends on original instinct, is not equally communicable to all men; and, so far as it depends on extended comparison, is unattainable by men employed in narrow fields of life" (16:144).

Whereas in "The Nature of Gothic" Ruskin had protested any "trenchant distinction of employment, as between idle and working men, or between men of liberal and illiberal professions" (10:201), he came now to urge a sharp distinction in the paths that led to employment—that is, in education. According to Ruskin's educational system, the upper and middle classes could become "good judges of Art" (16:182), but as for the worker of the lower class, "the less he knows [about Art] the better" (16:183). Earlier, Ruskin had declared it his central ambition "to spread the love and knowledge of art among all classes," and had joined in the founding of the Arundel Society (1848) to publish affordable color lithographs of Old Master paintings.[11]

Now, however, with his head swarming with the unbidden dreams and evil visions of his mental illness, and with what Robin Ironside has justly called his "defenseless and voracious sensibility" stretched taut (8), Ruskin acutely felt the danger and debility lurking within all unlimited visual experience. At best, his attempts somehow to exclude or to limit the flood of uncircumcised images that he now found alternately so exalting or so debasing represented a keen insight into the sensuous economy. At worst, however, they seemed to enact a willed constriction or scarification of human capacities. Without God as the ultimate and sanctifying end of art and beauty, Ruskin could not risk, so it seemed, any open-ended and purposeless role for them. The implicit selfishness he associated with art for art's sake, the surging sensuality he saw in the newer art of France and felt rampant in his own sexual nightmares, were simply too powerful, too dangerous to be allowed such scope, especially among the young, the uneducated, and the foolish.

By the 1860s, in turn, when Ruskin had begun addressing himself to the grinding social and economic problems that were destroying England—hunger, poverty, exploitation, greed—he found he had lost his audience. Specifically, he found himself imprisoned by his audience's expectation that he would pronounce exclusively upon art. Ruskin had thus succeeded in opening the eyes of this audience only to discover that they had closed their ears—and hearts and purses—against him. With such works as *Unto This Last* (1860) and *Munera Pulveris* (1862–63), his repudiation of the moral optimism inherent in the Whig aesthetic tradition strained and then broke the compact of liberal aspiration between Ruskin and his readers. The individuality that he had so generously nurtured in them—that appeal to their imaginative sense of themselves as endowed souls—rose up in its invigorated confidence to resist his call for subordination and self-sacrifice, while their aggressive new optimism scorned his own vehement despair. Ruskin's teachings in effect convinced his middle-class audiences that they had become culturally confident enough to reject the teacher himself.

In this way the wish for wide aesthetic influence that Ruskin had once made as a snappish young man was now unexpectedly fulfilled. Yet he found that the wishes of the young may become the nightmares of the old. The unbearable symbol of the contrast between what Ruskin had once wished and what he now wanted was Victorian Gothic. Everywhere—as if it meant to press his own pride and folly against his own optic nerve—the Gothic architecture he had championed twenty years before as the single style best suited to England and to serve as a "law" to all art (*Works,* 8:255), now assaulted his eyes. "No book of mine has had so much influence," as he said in 1874 on the publication of the third edition of *Stones of Venice,* but "I would rather, for my own part, that no architects had ever condescended to adopt one of the views suggested in this book, than that any should have made the partial use of it which has mottled our manufactory chimneys with black and red brick, dignified our banks and drapers' shops with Venetian tracery, and pinched our parish churches into dark and slippery arrangements for the advertisement of cheap coloured glass and pantiles" (9:11). The vital two-thirds of *Stones of Venice*—the "relation of the art of Venice to her moral temper, which is the chief subject of the book, and that of the life of the workman to his work, which is the most important practical principle developed in it" (9:14)—had gone unheeded, while the minutiae of Venetian Gothic ornament had become a new gospel, pored over, misunderstood, misapplied, and, worst of all, given material embodiment in the greasy, striated monstrosities of the "streaky bacon style" (10:lvi). These "accursed Frankenstein monsters of, *in*directly, my own making (10:459)" drove him to sell his house at Denmark Hill and buy another in the distant Lake Country.

Against this background, the libel trial of *Whistler v. Ruskin* came to assume the dimensions of a symbolic episode. Retreating into a natural landscape far removed not simply from the enormous, expanding, smoky city of London but also from the detestable commodifications and coteries of the new metropolitan art market, Ruskin sought to enact his intensifying conviction that all modern art merely diagnosed the fatal malaise of Victorian society and lacked utterly any power to heal it. Looking out at the London art world from Brantwood, the house in the Lake Country he purchased in 1871, Ruskin surveyed a domain that seemed to be shaped out of premises diametrically opposed to his own and whose grasping, self-promoting presumption was embodied in J. A. M. Whistler. A deracinated American and adoptive Parisian, Whistler was familiar with the cafés and ateliers of France and scorned the aesthetic preeminence given nature and literature over painting in England. His intense combativeness was matched in 1877 only by his economic vulnerability.[12]

When Ruskin attacked Whistler's painting *Nocturne in Black and Gold* in the July 1877 issue of his monthly letter to workingmen, *Fors Clavigera,* he was attacking, as many Victorians realized, the most Turneresque among recent paintings. Linda Merrill has argued that Ruskin may even have feared that "Whistler's unfocused pictures were an unconscious, or perhaps impertinent, imitation of Turner's grand manner," constituting in some sense simulated pictures that might delude an unwary public trained by Ruskin himself to idolize Turner (52). At the same time, there were decisive differences between the artist Ruskin had once so notably defended and the one he now so implacably attacked. For Whistler's nature is urbanized, his subject "low,"[13] and his color dull. Ruskin had for many years made his emphatic opinions known on precisely these questions, urging architects to move out of cities to build "true" buildings, broadcasting his contempt of Rembrandt and the Dutch painters for painting "stupid boors," and asserting that "pure" color was the safest guide to artistic talent and artistic truth. Whistler, by contrast, was exploring an evanescent, demotic, indeterminate realm that lay between—and thus blurred—the categories of city and country, noble and ignoble, that Ruskin was now desperately trying to keep clear. This indeterminate terrain of neutral tones, subjective impressions, and fragmentary effects would serve as the high road to twentieth-century modernism.

Yet such specifically artistic issues lie merely on the surface of Ruskin's angry response to Whistler's painting. For Ruskin's intense moral disdain for the American artist reverberates through the extended denunciation of Whistler in *Fors Clavigera.*[14] "Ill-educated conceit," "wilful imposture," "Cockney impudence," "coxcomb"—Ruskin's epithets belonged to the vocabulary of outraged civility adopted by the English moral community when it feels that its constitutive values (tolerance, unselfishness, sociability) have been assaulted.

Ruskin raises this larger point with his contrast between the gentle Edward Burne-Jones and the aggressive, self-advertising Whistler. For Burne-Jones's intensely individual paintings are, like Whistler's, subdued in color and lacking in "finish"; they, too, alienated a considerable portion of the Victorian public. But Ruskin believed that Burne-Jones's faults and eccentricities arose simply as the unavoidable costs of his sincere aims as a painter. Whistler's eccentricities, by contrast, proceeded out of his desire to astonish and intimidate, his idiosyncrasies epitomizing "the idolatry of the self in modern art" (Beatty, 38). In Ruskin's eyes, this unsubdued and unscrupulous egoism posed a pernicious threat to the social whole.

This is why Ruskin's original title for his *Fors* essay—"The Social Monster"—retains, as Merrill has noted, a special bearing upon their conflict (48). The phrase originally intended to describe a man solely motivated by money now came to apply to Whistler as artist, driven by the greed characteristic of so many Americans but impelled even more destructively by an animus against the free realm of human sociality itself. For beyond whatever may have been Whistler's opportunistic attempts to prey upon the gullibilities of the art public, Ruskin sensed in Whistler a deeper hostility to the claims and usages of civil society, the indispensable realm of judgment and interchange where, for Ruskin as for Carlyle, "man first becomes what he can be" and where the pending fate of nations is made manifest in their arts.

Yet there has always remained a sense in which the two symbolically opposed figures of Ruskin and Whistler, invested so heavily by both Victorian and modern commentators with every sort of contrasting meaning—old and new, rich and poor, establishmentarian and avant-gardist—can be found to have finally assumed positions not very different from one another. In his long retreat from the confident aesthetic hopes of *Stones of Venice,* Ruskin had reached a position very close to Whistler's own: both men deplored the growth of the art market and the art public as calamities for art, both doubted that aesthetic judgment was a universally shared capacity, both were driven by the public's disregard to eccentricity and half-crazed self-pity.

His darting, malicious speech salted with epigrams and with French when the epigrams failed, Whistler had reached his own views on art and the aesthetic by following the distinctly separate tradition of aesthetic thought that had developed in France. Friedrich Schiller's powerful belief in the sociocultural regenerativity to be found in the fine arts and in "aesthetic education" had been imported into France by Benjamin Constant and Victor Cousin, only to be transformed under the hard, utilitarian hand of the Saint-Simonians into the crudest sort of moralistic instrumentality. This capture of art and the aesthetic by the Saint-Simonian bureaucrats of the July revolution of 1830 had provoked in its turn a correspondingly extreme reaction—Théophile Gautier's notorious preface to *Mademoiselle de Maupin* (1834). This triumphant piece of provocation would become the manifesto of the *l'art pour l'art* aesthetics of ressentiment, supplying the polemical armory not merely for Charles Baudelaire and Stéphane Mallarmé but for Whistler and A. C. Swinburne and later for Wilde.

Ruskin, by contrast, had traveled a quite different path before reaching his gloomy conclusions about the state of public taste and its capacity for art and beauty. Nonetheless, as if roused by a vision of that expansive earlier hope published a quarter century before in *Stones of Venice,* Ruskin rallied to the defense of art understood as a socially redemptive power and attacked Whistler, who declared with barbed insouciance, "Listen! There never was an artistic period. There never was an Art-loving nation" (*Gentle Art,* 139). Galled by the crassly philistine reductionism that had converted art in England into a moral instrument of the state and identifying that reductionism specifically with Ruskin, who seemed to predominate everywhere as the famous Slade Professor of Art at Oxford, Whistler persuaded himself that he was attacking English philistinism by bringing his libel suit. In this way he might explode "the fabled link between the grandeur of Art and the glories and virtues of the State" (Whistler, 155) and discredit the man who had with such unwearied assiduity hammered the link home among the Victorians.

It is a salient irony of their extraordinary contest that Whistler, who ever argued for the superiority and absolute autonomy of the artist, turned for help in enforcing that claim precisely to the coercive machinery of the state. Specifically, he turned to the institution of the law, where the disabling distinctions—in income, in eminence, in audience—between himself and his rival would be effaced. Whistler without question required this equality before the law. He claimed that he had been harmed through nothing other than Ruskin's unequaled eminence as an art critic, and his counsel effectively dramatized this argument before the jury by characterizing Ruskin as a remote and irresponsible figure, "seated upon his throne of art," "a despot," saying what he pleased (Merrill, 185, 187). "There is no reason," the barrister solemnly told the jury, why Ruskin should "exercise his great powers of criticism and bring down all the influence he has gained in order to crush, and ruin, a comparatively struggling man" (184).

Yet Whistler was in fact asking something more of the law than justice and reparation—something, indeed, that the law was unable to provide. For Whistler hoped for a brilliantly public occasion on which to arraign and indict Ruskin's competence as an art critic. "The position of Mr. Ruskin as an art authority," as he would later say with scathing irony, "we left quite unassailed during the trial. To have said that Mr. Ruskin's pose among intelligent men, as other than a *littérateur* is false and ridiculous, would have been an invitation to the stake; and to be burnt alive, or stoned before the verdict, was not what I came into court for" (*Gentle Art,* 26). In addition to urgently needing £1,000, Whistler sought to challenge Ruskin's intolerable tyranny as an art critic.

Denied any financial relief by the jury's award of a contemptuous farthing's worth of damages, and denied the momentous courtroom drama he had hoped for by Ruskin's failure to appear at the trial,[15] Whistler rewrote their conflict more satisfactorily, first in a pamphlet published a month after the trial and later in his famous book, *The Gentle Art of Making Enemies* (1892). In these pages *Whistler v. Ruskin* came to stand for the war "between the brush and the pen" (*Gentle Art,* 25), between practicing artists whose genuine authority flowed from their ability to create art and the nonpracticing critics who gained spurious authority because their "dicta are *printed as law*" in newspapers and books (31; emphasis added). In making such a distinction, Whistler almost appears to appeal to a quasi-democratic model of aesthetic discourse, insisting that the authority claimed by such critics as Ruskin is illegitimate because they do not represent the activity they control and then proposing to replace such empty authoritarianism with the genuine authority of artists who practice what they preach.

In the end, however, Whistler's gesture was more a tactical move than a sincere motive. He wished to sweep the board clean of competitors so that he could establish in the evacuated space the absolute authoritativeness—the "sole authority" and law—of the artist (Whistler, 32). Instead of the civic exercise of "judging for yourself," Whistler demanded that aesthetic judgment be "based upon laws as rigid and defined as those of the known sciences" (32). Instead of the reciprocally civilizing and humanizing interchanges of public taste, he insisted that the artwork "be received in silence" (30).

Whistler's operative model, then, had become one of specialist knowledge and professional expertise, not aesthetic democracy. As he informed the presiding judge at the trial, "I should not disapprove in any way of technical criticism by a man whose life is passed in the practice of the science that he criticizes; but for the opinion of a man whose life is not so passed I would have as little opinion as you would have if he expressed an opinion on the law. I hold that none but an artist can be a competent critic" (Merrill, 148). In his polemical effort to protect the professional prerogatives of the artist, Whistler now turned upon the absurd accomplice he saw lurking behind the usurping critic: the democratic masses. The millenium of public taste, Whistler sneered, would be accomplished by a simple scheme:

> *The galleries are to be thrown open on Sundays, and the public, dragged from their beer to the British Museum, are to delight in the Elgin Marbles, and appreciate what the early Italians have done to elevate their thirsty souls! An inroad into the laboratory would be looked upon as an intrusion; but before the triumphs of Art, the expounder is at his ease, and points out the doctrine that Raphael's results are within the reach of any beholder,*[16] *provided he enrol himself with Ruskin or hearken to [Sidney] Colvin [Slade Professor of Art at Cambridge] in the provinces. The people are to be educated upon the broad basis of "Taste," forsooth, and it matters but little what "gentleman and scholar" undertake the task.* (32–33)

Whistler had earlier been driven to all his spuriously aristocratic poses—West Point officer, St. Petersburg prince, Southern cavalier, white supremacist[17]—by the raw social and commercial frictions of Jacksonian America and Second Empire France. As he ridiculed art critics, denied any possibility of their legitimate function, and sneered at the public unless it submitted to silence and to law, Whistler did nothing less than fracture the socio-aesthetic sphere premised by the Whig aesthetic tradition as the crucial domain of citizenship. Here it is that, high and low, learned and unlearned, the people in their liberty learned to judge for themselves and to partake of delights that are, as Colvin himself had said, "at once the most communicable and the most inalienable, the most open for all to share and the most impossible for anything to take away" (591).

Preferring *technē* to all *theoria,* however, Whistler now turned instead to appeal in vague gestures to a new aristocracy of expertise, a sort of technological elite of practicing specialists whose strands of filiation clearly trailed backwards to the Saint-Simonians themselves and forward to the dreadful, dehumanizing bureaucracies of the twentieth century. Imagine, Whistler imperiously demanded, "the College of Physicians with Tennyson as President!" (33) and you will have the revolting absurdity of a school of art headed by a mere *littérateur* such as Ruskin: the institution of art, he asserted, can only be headed by artists.

In this moment of direct assault on aesthetic democracy and "judging for yourself," one might expect to see rise in defense of such ideals a Ruskin who would champion the claims of the moral-aesthetic realm, the *sensus communis,* and Aristotle's "energy of contemplation"—the critic whose continuous stream of compelling aesthetic judgments had almost alone taught Victorians how to see art and nature and to see them in their profoundest social ramifications. Yet this Ruskin is curiously absent from *Whistler v. Ruskin,* just as Ruskin himself was absent from the actual Exchequer Chamber courtroom in which the trial occurred.

Ruskin refused to frame his defense against Whistler in terms of the *sensus communis* or the social whole. He turned instead to the authoritarian fiction that had haunted him all his life: the idea of law. "The Bench of honourable Criticism," Ruskin declared in his instructions to his defense counsel, "is as truly a Seat of Judgment as that of Law itself" (Merrill, 290). Ruskin stubbornly based his defense on the claim that he was justified in defaming Whistler because, as Ruskin told his lawyers, "the description given of him is *absolutely true*" (291; emphasis added). He refused to consider his lawyers' urgent appeal to sanction the other defense possible under the circumstances—the defense of "fair comment." As Francis L. Fennell has outlined the legal consequences involved, the justification defense was much harder to adopt in a case of this kind, "since it required the defendant to prove that he was *right* in what he said." In a defense of fair comment, by contrast, "one simply had to establish that his opinion *could be shared by other competent and temperate judges,* whether or not his judgment was in the abstract 'correct'" (18; emphasis added).

Ruskin could have won on the basis of a fair-comment defense. Critics had for years been complaining about the slight labor involved in Whistler's canvases, so that even Ruskin's fierce and notorious phrase "flinging a pot of paint in the public's face" might have been taken as a reasonable exaggeration of the artist's hasty and off-hand approach to his work—a comment made in the interest of protecting the public and hence constituting fair comment. This is why Ruskin's refusal to sanction such a defense assumes momentous symbolic weight. For in rejecting the defense of fair comment, Ruskin rejects the public sphere of sociability—the recognized Whig domain of mutually enhancing moral exchange and judging for oneself, with its trust in the common judgment of ordinary people and its optimistic faith that such judgment communicated at some level with a realm of transcendental value.

By insisting on a legal defense of justification, Ruskin signaled his desire to win his own vindication as an individual detached from the public sphere—a crown of imperishable authority and right that would descend to him alone from the ghostly Platonic paradigm of law he had pursued at every step of his career. For example, in the preface of volume 1 of *Modern Painters,* he declared, "Whatever I have asserted throughout the work, I have endeavoured to ground altogether on demonstrations" that "ought to involve no more reference to authority or character than a demonstration in Euclid" (*Works,* 3:5); in his middle years, he declared that work "*has* a worth just as fixed and real as the specific gravity of a substance" (17:67); and in the September 1877 *Fors Clavigera,* where Ruskin quoted page after page from the *Laws* of Plato. Thus, in the end, "law" became less a figure for order and regularity for Ruskin than a metaphor for his own unmediated access to authoritarian certainty and to the even more ancient realm of aristocratic preeminence and absolutist divine right.

Perhaps only looking back at the *Whistler v. Ruskin* trial from a perspective well beyond it, however, does it become possible to see the degree to which the courtroom drama reflected a conflict still more profound. For operating at a distance from any of the specific disputes about defamation or damages is the implicit ontological conflict between the traditional belief in the external order of reality entailed by the ontic logos and a newer belief in an inner order or energy of nature within each individual subject.

Repeatedly, in the court testimony and again in the press coverage of *Whistler v. Ruskin,* the conventional awareness that aesthetic preferences vary, that "there is no accounting for tastes," is to be found verging upon quite another feeling—a sense that such variations may themselves represent or constitute a deeper nature or reality within. "As to what the picture represents," Whistler informs Ruskin's defense counsel, "that depends upon who looks at it" (Merrill, 151), and such a declaration sounds the distinctive note of the expressivist turn (Taylor, *Sources,* 389), with its subordination of external reality to the truth of an inward nature or vision. "*Nocturne in Black and Gold* was not painted to offer the portrait of a particular place," Whistler told his own counsel, "but as an artistic impression that had been carried away" from the scene (154).

Whistler's nocturnes—ludicrous, mysterious, evocative, notorious—would serve as a sort of proximate Victorian site for the increasingly palpable authenticity of this inward and individual reality. A few years earlier, Frederic Harrison had advised the readers of the *Fortnightly Review* that "We must reason and act *as if* there were an external world, and as if there were, and we could know, general and constant laws." In the face of this increasingly provisional outward realm, the more significant truth would become that "everything depends on our recognising as the substratum of our philosophy, that all knowledge is relative; relative in respect of its having no absolute certainty, and relative as respects its harmonising with the mental and moral nature of man" ("Subjective Synthesis," 197).

This diminution and eventual virtual disappearance, under conditions of postmodernism, of the outward world external to the self would come to constitute what Luc Ferry has called *le retrait du monde* (23). Among the late Victorians, the steady withdrawal of the realm of objective experience before an accelerating subjectivization of the world could be perceived only intermittently or partially through such openings into the new inward world as were offered by artworks like Whistler's impressions. Wilde makes this point in *The Decay of Lying* (1889), when his witty protagonist demands, "To whom, if not to [the Impressionists] and their master [i.e., Whistler], do we owe the lovely silver mists that brood over our river, and turn to faint forms of fading grace curved bridge and swaying barge?" For Whistler's impressionist nocturnes show the external world in the very process of disappearing or "harmonising with the mental and moral nature of man." "Things are because we see them," Wilde's protagonist concludes, and sagely insists his real point has all along been a "metaphysical" one (*Critic as Artist,* 312).

When Ruskin's defense lawyer asked the artist Albert Moore if Whistler's nocturnes were not full of "eccentricity," Moore responded firmly, "I should call it 'originality'" (Merrill, 159). Precisely this reinterpretation of eccentricity as originality, however, provides a glimpse the expanding authoritativeness of the inward and individual vision as it confronted the older notion of an outward and universal order of being, where persons, events, and ideas occupied ascertainable positions (e.g., "eccentric" vs. "central") that were clear when viewed against a "publically available background" (Taylor, *Sources,* 491). With the diminution of this publicly available background and the gradual impoverishment of the idea of what Harrison had called "general and constant laws"—the idea of law to which both Ruskin and Whistler had appealed—the metaphysical ground assumed and indeed required by the Whig aesthetic tradition, as by the political liberalism lying beyond it, would narrow and become problematic.

At the time, however, such discursive categories and tensions were far too close at hand and constitutive of ordinary experience to be readily visible to most Victorians. It was much easier and more comprehensible to displace any vagrant intimations of discursive tension or anomaly onto the painful and pathetic spectacle of Ruskin mad. For here the conflict between the order of the ontic logos and that of the inward vision, if it was felt at all, could assume a human scale and meaning. As the obtrusions of his mental disease became ever more devastating and importunate, the spectacle of Ruskin railing against a frightful modernity where the canals of Venice were filled with the "green tide . . . of floating corpses" (*Works,* 28:757), and the skies of England were darkened with "The Storm Cloud of the Nineteenth Century" (1884) seemed to many Victorians to represent nothing less than the drama of a man who had tragically lost or willfully abandoned his connection to the reliably available external world. Ruskin's vehement "contempt for public opinion," as W. J. Courthope observed sadly in 1880, linked him unmistakably to "the followers of art for art's sake" ("Progress," 72).

If, by contrast, precisely the titanically distraught and visionary Ruskin of *Fors Clavigera* and the other late works has in recent years most engaged modern critical attention, his Victorian inheritors could find no acknowledged place for this Ruskin. Instead, it seemed clear to them that the man who first opened the way to the most persuasive account of a life lived in art remained at the end unincluded in the ideal he had so richly imagined. This is why Ruskin, "brought up," in Harrison's words, "as a kind of Dalai Lama, veiled from touch or sight of the world without" (*John Ruskin,* 195), the Graduate of Oxford who, in the opinion of Jowett of Balliol, "has never rubbed his mind against others, so that he is ignorant of very obvious things" (2:257), even in his final isolation—precisely because of his final isolation—would compel the renewed search for utopian community by Morris, Pater, and Wilde, who, in quarreling with Ruskin, would reassert the Victorian argument for aesthetic democracy.

The Brotherly Company of Art

I want the democracy of the arts established: I want every one to think for himself about them, and not to take things for granted from hearsay; every man to do what he thinks right, not in anarchical fashion, but feeling that he is responsible to his fellows for what he feels, thinks, and has determined.

(Morris, "The Lesser Arts of Life")

AMONG THE GREAT Victorians devoting themselves to questions of art, William Morris stands forth as the supreme champion of aesthetic democracy. At the midpoint of his career, he called for what he termed the "the democracy of the arts," by which he meant an equalization of respect paid to the fine and the applied arts. Morris's ambition, however, extended much further. His object, as one friend described it, "was none other than the democratisation of beauty. He had sojourned in the House Beautiful, and now he wished everyone to live there" (Compton-Rickett, 21).

This larger ambition impelled him to seek not simply a local set of decorative arrangements or artistic relations but the sociopolitical ideal I have been calling aesthetic democracy—that utopian social transformation by which the unanimous yet uncoerced bond between the citizens and their polity approximated the relation between aesthetic perceivers and the beautiful. Here life would at last realize the promise Morris had for so long seen manifest only in art: to be "shared by gentle and simple, learned and unlearned, and be as a language that all can understand" (*Works,* 22:165). Morris thus strove continually so "that the *Arts* might be re-created and knit together into one vital organic Art, filling the whole of life. And he strove that *the people* be re-created and knit together into one vital organic commonwealth" (Tanner, 10).

Morris launched himself on the crusade to establish aesthetic democracy when he went up to Oxford in 1853, read Ruskin's "Nature of Gothic," and felt, in the words of his great biographer J. W. Mackail, "an admiration akin to worship" (1:220). Ruskin's Gothic ideal struck Morris with the force of revelation because it gave voice to exactly Morris's own inward experience of beauty, a pleasure so puissant that he believed it was operating at the most fundamental level of human experience. Ruskin's liberal Gothic ideal confirmed what Morris already knew—that an "instinct for beauty . . . is inborn in every complete man" (*Works,* 23:168) and, therefore, that art is "a positive necessity of life" (22:53). If this instinct had been cruelly blighted by the withering conditions of industrial modernity, Morris became convinced after reading Ruskin that it could nonetheless be restored by a passionate and concerted effort, a commitment representing nothing less than a "Crusade and Holy Warfare against the age" (Mackail, 1:63).

Morris's epiphany at Oxford thus represents the proximate moment when art first became available to Victorians as a moral source, "the love of which empowers us to do and be good" (Taylor, *Sources,* 93). Precisely with Morris's generation, rising after the middle of the nineteenth century, opened up the two moral horizons that came to serve late Victorians in Britain and America as alternatives to belief in God: the scientistic ethic of unbelief adopted by such figures as Leslie Stephen, Thomas Huxley, and Samuel Butler and the Romantic ideal of self-completion through art followed by Morris, Walter Pater, and Oscar Wilde (Taylor, *Sources,* 408–9).

Morris's great significance to his own and subsequent generations is that he instantiated this notion of art as a moral source in an actual life. Owing to a set of unusual circumstances—in particular, his complete financial independence at the age of twenty-one due to the early death of his wealthy father—Morris could live his life in art on the most attractive terms.[1] Combining youth, genius, idealism, and passion, Morris's exemplary life exerted a powerful formative influence on succeeding generations of artistically ambitious young men and women, from Pater and Wilde in England to Gustave Stickley and Candace Wheeler in America. "If some angel offered me the choice," as W. B. Yeats said well into the twentieth century, "I would choose to live [Morris's] life, poetry and all, rather than my own or any other man's" (*Autobiography,* 95).

Art became a moral source for Morris at the moment he realized from reading Ruskin that his own intense response to beauty was not merely shared by others but was in fact universal. Like Ruskin, Morris possessed what John D. Rosenberg has eloquently called a "chastity of recall" (221) through which a first vision of a beautiful church or natural scene remains perfectly clear and undiminished even fifty years after seeing it. Yet Morris's visual ecstasy—what George Levine in another context has called "the almost mindless physicality" of an engagement with beauty (4)—differed significantly from Ruskin's in that the pleasure of both seeing and producing beauty affected him somatically, not merely as a frisson along the skin but in his body's very core. "I always know when a thing is really good," Morris later told his friend Sydney Olivier when the two were examining illuminated manuscripts, "by its making me feel warm across here"; Morris rubbed "with both hands that part of his waistcoat that covered the seat of his diaphragm" (Olivier, 440).

In the same way, the architect and designer W. R. Lethaby would recall Morris working on the border designs for the Kelmscott *Chaucer* in a virtual trance of kineaesthetic pleasure, the graphic forms being "*stroked* into place, as it were, with a sensation like that of smoothing a cat." To express this sensuous pleasure, Lethaby remembered, Morris "used to say that all good designing was felt in the stomach" (Sparling, 67). From his earliest experiences as a schoolboy, ceaselessly working his netting amidst the clamor and brutality of the Marlborough College schoolroom, Morris identified his visceral experience of making and seeing art not with the "free play" of the higher cognitive faculties characteristic of Aristotle's "energy of contemplation" or Immanuel Kant's aesthetic judgment but with the soothing and inspiriting physical play of unbridled animals.[2]

At the same time, the physical emotion that Morris felt in perceiving beauty as well as the "unreasoning, sensuous pleasure in handiwork" that he felt when producing it (*Works,* 23:174) convinced him that his own absorbingly somatic response to art and beauty must constitute a universal condition among all perceivers, one that transcended the accidents of birth, fortune, or education by operating through the immanent democracy of the body. Morris's deep responsiveness to beauty seemed to him so obviously to operate on the entirely demotic level of physical process, the level of respiration and digestion, of adrenalation and fatigue, that he could not imagine that everyone did not experience it. Following his own habit of generalizing, as he put it, "from the only specimen of humanity of which I know anything; to wit, myself" (23:81), Morris did not hesitate to attribute his own feelings to everyone else.

If in this moment of ardent generalization the extraordinary nature of his own aesthetic response tended to disappear from view, it was simultaneously the moment in which beauty understood as the "pleasure of the eyes" and art understood as the "pleasurable exercise of our energies" would suggest themselves to Morris not simply as the ideal model of human labor but as a possible model for the ideal society in which such labor might take place. Upon this basis of sensuous pleasure, then, generously if unwittingly deduced from his own highly singular constitution, Morris raised his utopian hopes for communal art and life.

To realize these hopes for a social world in which beauty was known as pleasure and known by all, Morris either founded or joined a series of brotherly companies, of which the best-known were the famous design firm of Morris and Company and the Socialist League. As each brotherly company was founded, it represented both an attempt to remedy the failures of the one that had preceded it and an expansion of Morris's hope for the transformative social ideal. As each company in its turn disappointed him, it marked the momentary contraction of Morris's hope for aesthetic democracy.

The formation of these brotherly companies was sustained at a deep level by another of Morris's uncommon personal gifts—his ability to merge himself into the social totality without suffering either anxiety or loss of identity. This seamless merging of the individual into the social whole, a process by which the envelope of personality remains at once intact yet permeable, is what Mackail meant by Morris's "innate Socialism" (1:338). This rare disposition of body and mind formed the basis for Morris's conviction that "the consciousness of each one that he belongs to a corporate body, working harmoniously, each for all, and all for each, will bring about real and happy equality" (*Works,* 22:374)—the conviction that in turn supplied the basis for his later commitment to socialism.

Yet by its very nature, a disposition to merge easily but with undiminished power into the communal life of the group tends to obscure the rarity of such a social gift, naturalizing it along with Morris's other gifts so as to render them invisible both to himself and to others. This phenomenon doubtless explains why Morris's older sisters thought reading came to him by "instinct," why Mackail thought Morris's love of the Middle Ages "born in him," and why his Oxford friends realized only very slowly how thoroughly and yet effortlessly Morris seemed to know things—"What an extraordinary power of observation lay at the base of many of his casual or incidental remarks, and how many things he knew that were quite out of our way" (Mackail, 1:10, 44).

At the same time, precisely this background of Morris's extraordinary personal gifts thrust into a new and salient visibility the repeating pattern of difficulties associated with his various artistic quests and brotherly companies. For Morris's recurrent and cumulative disappointments finally suggested to some of his followers, if not to Morris himself, exactly the possibility long ago identified by Bernard Mandeville that an exceptional or aristocratic sensibility, generously or deludedly, projects its own extraordinary gifts on ordinary humankind as a universal capacity shared by all, high and low, learned and unlearned. If the plenitude of Morris's imaginative and artistic endowments tended to obscure from him the rarity and contingency of his own gifts, such lesser men as William Holman Hunt were not similarly disadvantaged. In time they came to wonder if an unlikely conjunction of social and personal circumstances had not led

Morris, so "sheltered," as Hunt remarked, "from real hardships in the struggle of life" (Sharp, 29), to repeat Shaftesbury's generous error of attributing to the many the capacities of the few.

Morris's transformative social ideal was indelibly colored by Oxford, where he arrived as an undergraduate at a crucial moment in 1853. By that date, the fierce theological passions of the Oxford Movement had subsided, leaving the air charged, as it seemed to the new generation, with an electric if amorphous expectancy. Oxford's long eighteenth-century sleep of spiritual somnolence and intellectual torpor had been broken, never to return; the university lay open to all the energies of change that surged within Oxford in the shape of university reform and beyond Oxford in the shape of political liberalism. This rising tide was swelled by such radical workers' movements as Chartism and the Continental revolutions of 1848 that would culminate in the Liberal Party victory of 1868 and William Ewart Gladstone's first tenure as prime minister.

In this expanding moment of liberal hopes, the physical presence of Oxford strongly shaped the dreams and idealisms of Morris and his friends. Oxford lay as yet unbreached by the forces of modernity: if the railroad grazed it lightly on one side, its common street architecture was still largely that of the fifteenth century. The "base and brickish skirt" of suburban housing that Gerard Manley Hopkins would later deplore in "Duns Scotus's Oxford" (1879) had not yet soured the city's gray beauty. Oxford at this time still boasted gray-roofed houses, a long winding street, and the sound of many bells, and Morris, like Ruskin's other ardent disciples, came there "as to some miraculous place, full of youthful enthusiasm, thirsting after knowledge and beauty" (Mackail, 1:31).

The years at Oxford, which Mackail characterizes as the aristocratic phase of Morris's life, mark a watershed in his subsequent career. For the Oxford of this time was to become the fixed standard against which he would measure first the visual degradation of Victorian England and later that of Oxford itself. "There are many places in England where a young man may get as good book-learning as in Oxford," Morris somberly declared in 1882, but "not one where he can receive the education which the loveliness of the grey city used to give us" (*Works,* 22:232). This bitter phrase marks the moment when Morris recognized that a Whiggery that could so cravenly and venally bungle away Oxford's irreplaceable beauty had lapsed into political illegitimacy. In November 1883, Morris made a point of returning to Oxford to announce that he had become "one of those called Socialists" (*Works,* 23:171).

In the hopeful mid-1850s, however, as Morris and his closest friend, Edward Burne-Jones, wandered the Oxford streets and spent their afternoons in Merton Chapel (built ca. 1275) or New College cloisters (built ca. 1385), they began to talk of founding a new conventual order or brotherhood with the money Morris had inherited upon reaching his majority. Morris's deeply historicist imagination had been molded by years of reading medieval history and archaeology and animated by the heady contemporary models of F. D. Maurice and Charles Kingsley's Christian socialism as well as the art fellowships of G. E. Street in England and the Nazarenes in Rome. Influenced by these forces, Morris and Burne-Jones devised a plan for a religious order—"the Order of Sir Galahad"—that soon modulated into a social brotherhood, the physical presence of Oxford working all the while to convince them that the medieval ideal of Ruskin's "Nature of Gothic" could in fact become wholly real.

The Order of Sir Galahad in turn modulated into the decorative arts firm Morris, Marshall, Faulkner and Company (1861): "The monastery of [Morris's] Oxford dreams rose into being as a workshop, and the Brotherhood became a firm registered under the Companies Acts" (Mackail, 1:144). Formed with such college friends as Burne-Jones and such friendly older artists as Ford Madox Brown and Dante Gabriel Rossetti, Morris, Marshall sought to carry the skill and taste of artists first into the Anglican Church—aided there by the contemporary movement toward ecclesiastical ornament and ceremony known as Ritualism—and later into the Victorian home. For once driven from the aesthetic Eden of Oxford, Morris and Burne-Jones had found themselves in the fallen world of ordinary Victorian visuality, where there was "not a chair, or table, or bed; not a cloth or paper hanging for the walls; nor tiles to line fireplaces or passages; nor a curtain or a candlestick; nor a jug to hold wine or a glass to drink it out of, but had to be reinvented, one might almost say, to escape the flat ugliness of the current article" (Mackail, 1:142).

Beyond the aim of creating beautiful domestic surroundings capable of enhancing the life lived in their midst, Morris believed that with the company he could contest "the system which insists on individualism and forbids co-operation" (*Works,* 23:167). He meant by this phrase the system of competitive commerce that was so deeply maiming both producers and consumers of art under the regime of Victorian capitalism. Morris resisted the call to produce unique artworks of the aristocratic tradition, which he identified with Rossetti's one-of-a-kind oil paintings, because he saw that such artworks had become enmeshed in the false scarcities, monopolies, and commodifications of the capitalist system. Instead, Morris chose to devote himself to the two-dimensional and repeating designs of his famous wallpapers, carpets, and fabrics. These infinitely reproducible—and theoretically mass-producible—goods were perfectly suited to the requirements of the democratic or mass market.

But there always persisted a sense in which Morris remained an unwitting prisoner of precisely the aristocratic assumptions he had overtly rejected. For Morris's self-sufficiency, his unquestioning belief in "individuality, which is the breath of life to art" (*Works,* 22:267), and, most of all, his imperious eye—which compelled him to prefer certain artistic proceedings over others because he knew them to be aesthetically right—constantly worked counter to the communal Gothic aesthetic he had for so long studied and admired and hoped so fervently to install in his workrooms.[3]

This unassailable certainty and proud refusal to compromise in artistic matters first impelled Morris to wrest control away from the larger art fellowship of Morris, Marshall, Faulkner, and Company and reconstitute it solely in himself as Morris and Company in 1875. Morris's imperious virtuosity then resurfaced in the new company, as if reexpressing in a Victorian register the hidden ground of aristocratic taste and virtuoso judgment that Shaftesbury had drawn upon in the eighteenth century to model the moral-aesthetic sense. Morris's artistic conscience thus repeatedly blocked full realization of the company's goals, bewildering him.

The contradiction first identified by Mandeville and later repressed within the Whig aesthetic tradition—the tension between the aristocratic basis and the democratic claims of the moral-aesthetic sense—thus repeatedly disrupted Morris's utopian hopes for social and artistic transformation or enmeshed them in crippling difficulties. In Morris's practice as an art designer and businessman, this tension or contradiction operated on two different levels. To understand the disruption it imparted to the production of art, it is useful to review Peter Floud's remarkable analysis of Morris's practice as a pattern designer. Grounded in the procedures of such designing, Floud's notably unsentimental account has more clearly than any other exposed the external and internal constraints continually pulling Morris's artistic practice away from his social and aesthetic principles.

As Morris himself constantly reminded his readers and listeners, his artistic principles derived from Ruskin's "Nature of Gothic." In a single leap of inspiration, Ruskin had grasped the two central principles of medieval art—first, that "the art of any epoch must of necessity be the expression of its social life," and second, that "the social life of the Middle Ages allowed the workman freedom of individual expression" (*Works,* 22:323). Like Ruskin himself, Morris invests the desires of the post-Enlightenment heart in a fiction of the pre-Enlightenment past, viewing the Gothic centuries in the same way as Friedrich Schiller and J. J. Winckelmann had regarded the Greek. These men saw the past as epochs of unmaimed and multiform wholeness—ancient Greece, in Schiller's eyes, existing as free of "our mutilated nature," just as the Middle Ages existed, for Morris, free of the "wretched lop-sided creatures we are being made by the excess of the division of labour in the occupations of life" (*Works,* 22:338).

Yet as Floud has made clear, Morris could neither evade this kind of modern disfigurement nor shield his workers from it. Instead, the nature of Morris's chosen medium (two-dimensional, predominantly repeating patterns) and his own individual nature (tireless, irascible, utterly independent) combined to prevent him from putting Ruskin's Gothic principles into commercial practice. On the one hand, Morris's wallpaper designs required of his workers "a type of niggling, mechanical, repetitive handwork altogether different from his picture of the happy medieval stonemason" because hand-block technique requires printing "one colour of the pattern over and over again down the long roll of paper, taking great care to see that each impression of the block exactly fits the next so that no joins are visible" (Floud, 616).

On the other hand, however, Morris's own exigent standards as a designer and manufacturer—"Since I am the designer of these things & know what I want, there can be no appeal against my judgement" (*Letters,* 2A:18)—made it impossible for him either to resign his supervision of the workers or to consider using machines for this tiring and repetitive work. As he told a manufacturing associate, "I don't think you should look forward to our *ever* using a machine" (*Letters,* 1:280). When this man later protested the "tyranny" to his workmen represented by such unyielding standards of excellence, Morris retorted, "I do not understand what you mean by tyranny to your workman: it is no tyranny to expect a printer to make his blocks register properly. . . . What I want you to understand is this, that my position depends entirely on my keeping up the excellence of my goods: the public know my pretensions in this matter, &, very properly, will not let me be worse than my word: and I am determined whatever may be the cost in all ways not to fail in it" (*Letters,* 2A:18).

Morris's language here is woven from the warp of commerce ("my position," "my goods") and the woof of romance, as Morris, determined "not to fail" and hewing to the sacred promise of "my word," soldiers on like Childe Roland "making his way on to his point through all dreadful things," as Morris once described Robert Browning's doggedly heroic knight (*Works,* 1:339). Here the "constant supervision" of the artist, first promised in the advertising brochure of Morris, Marshall, Faulkner, and Company (Mackail, 1:151), took on a dismaying new meaning of quasi-tyrannical superintendence, while the principles of cooperation and association among art workers also advertised in those pages seemed to slip from view. To such artistic contemporaries as Walter Crane, Morris's importance as a designer derived from precisely this mode of stringent supervision.[4] But Crane's view of Morris poses a double difficulty.

First, to the degree that it is true, it distances Morris's practice from Ruskin's Gothic ideal of free individual expression and the providential imperfection of ordinary workers' work. Second, however, it is not especially true—Floud estimates that Morris supervised less than 50 percent of his own designs (616).

This is why Floud reluctantly concludes that Morris's artistic practice not only had less effect on art manufactures than has been traditionally claimed for it but also that its effect was less socially beneficent than Morris's own principles tended to suggest. In fact, the social and moral benefits that both Ruskin and Morris identified in handwork are nowhere to be found in Morris's actual procedures: hand printing Morris's wallpapers did not provide his workmen with opportunities for greater freedom, delicacy, or initiative. Its advantage was wholly technical and aesthetic—hand printing wallpaper allows a slower application of colors and therefore richer, more opaque hues. Instead, the single unperplexed message arising from Morris's actual practice as a designer and a supervisor of designs becomes that of his all-denying, individualist devotion to the work at hand and to the aristocratic ideal of craftsmanship he had first learned from Rossetti.

If Morris's intense pleasure in creating art thus tended to disguise from himself the degree to which his utopian hopes were constrained and compromised by his practice in the production of art,[5] however, this did not occur on the level of art consumption. For here, by contrast, Morris realized with a daily growing indignation that art had come not to relieve but instead to poison the class wound. Deformed by competitive commerce, art no longer served as "the one certain solace of labour" (*Works,* 23:279). Instead, it was now widening "that fatal division of men into the cultivated and the degraded classes" (*Letters,* 2A:173). With the extinction of the authentic art of the people, the aesthetic impulse in Victorian times lived merely a "poor thin life among a few exceptional men," while it taught those same men to despise "those beneath them for an ignorance for which they themselves are responsible, for a brutality that they will not struggle with" (*Works,* 22:26).

For this reason, Morris's response to the movement launched so largely under his influence—the Arts and Crafts Movement of the 1880s and 1890s—was deeply conflicted and ambivalent. Seeking to close such class divisions with the tools and camaraderie of the artisanal workroom, the Arts and Crafts Movement, as Peter Stansky has argued, repeatedly found itself instead paralyzed and riven by the very anxieties of gentility it had sought to transcend, in the end becoming, as one of its founders declared somberly, "a narrow and tiresome little aristocracy working with great skill for the very rich" (Harris, 342).

Thus, in the midst of the most concerted effort to bring the first tokens of aesthetic democracy into ordinary Victorian houses, Morris saw the resurgence of aristocratic pride and opulence recontaining the democratic hope and expressing it in a plutocratic fantasy of the "simple life"—in exquisite ceramics, hand-painted medieval settles, costly webs of embroidered silk tapestry. Morris, Marshall and Company's first advertising brochure boldly asserted that "good decoration, involving rather the luxury of taste than the luxury of costliness, will be found to be much less expensive than is generally supposed" (Mackail, 1:152). This facile opposition between a "luxury of taste" and a "luxury of costliness," however, worked only further to mystify the central questions with which Morris, Marshall and later Morris and Company would so continually struggle. Could an art fellowship produce marketable goods? Could a brotherly company remain brotherly when constituted under the Companies Acts? Could ordinary people afford this luxury of taste? Morris was quick to refuse to participate in an 1881 exhibition that would have segregated designs for workers' cottages from those for gentlemen's houses, declaring, "I will have nothing to do with anything, however good the intention, which to my mind tends to keep up the division of classes" (*Letters,* 2A:12).

Yet such invidious class distinctions did not by themselves disable Morris's Gothic ideal of democratic art, which dictated that "what furniture a workman can buy should be *exactly* the same (if his room be big enough) as a lord buys" (*Letters,* 2A:12). For as a merely practical matter, Morris recognized that as long as sturdy well-made furniture was constructed for workers as he wished it to be made—without machines—it would "not cost twice as much" as the wretched deal pieces they now used, "but twenty times as much: crede mihi experte" (*Letters,* 2A:17).

Thus, despite twenty years as a craftsman devoted to the "lesser arts" of the ordinary domestic sphere, Morris would never see the luxury of costliness replaced by that modest ideal of aesthetic democracy, the luxury of taste. Instead, driven by his own high and implacable standard of craftsmanship, which would not allow the tawdry approximations produced by machine manufacture, Morris watched helplessly as the democratic ideal of a luxury of taste was wholly absorbed and recontained within a crassly plutocratic luxury of costliness.[6]

To the degree that Morris attempted to solve this difficulty he did so by urging a radical simplification of life upon the plutocratic customers his unyielding aesthetic forced him to serve. His message to the genteel classes would thus become "do with as little furniture, as little ornament, as you possibly can" (*Letters,* 2A:17). Stifled by the crammed, airless, overupholstered respectabilities of late-Victorian luxury, he urged and sought himself a simplicity of interior design that he called Spartan, his friends considered primitive,[7] and we may recognize as deriving from the same liberating Stoic simplicity that Shaftesbury had once hoped to place at the center of the Whig polity. Yet precisely this sincerity involved Morris in an absurd contradiction: called upon to give his decorating advice to important clients in person, Morris longed to say what he really believed: "Don't decorate at all: whitewash it all" (May Morris, 2:616).

Even this failure of his aesthetic ideal on the level of consumption might have been bearable, however, had it not been for Morris's crushing sense of living in an "age ridden by the nightmare of commercial ugliness" (*Unpublished Lectures,* 78), in which art at last showed itself to be impotent before "all this filth of civilization" (*Works,* 23:280). As Morris looked around, he saw that art had become powerless before the anarchic onslaught of modern civilization, whether that assault was "the spreading sore of London swallowing up with its loathsomeness field and wood and heath" (23:207), "the black horror and reckless squalor of our manufacturing districts, so dreadful to the senses" (23:207), the "degradation that has so speedily befallen" Oxford (23:171), or simply the inescapable dull squalor of jerry-built suburban villas and shop windows crammed with "miserable trumpery" (23:195).

Although Morris worked actively through the Society for the Protection of Ancient Buildings to stem some of the damage, he felt, with Ruskin, that the forces he opposed—swarming, autonomous, seemingly relentless—verged on the demonic. He faced the "putrid sea" of modern ugliness (22:337)—"the filthy modern tide," as his young admirer W. B. Yeats would later call it in his poem "The Statues"—but like King Canute, Morris felt himself sitting deedless: "The stream of civilization is against us, and we cannot battle against it" (22:38). Even the image of Canute resisting the tide was too noble for the dull and eyeless squalor Morris most feared, and he later exchanged this image for another: England would become nothing more than a countinghouse on top of a cinder heap (23:280).

Sickened by the resistless process of degradation through which industrial capitalism traded the golden world of medieval wealth—its pleasure of the eyes, its sympathy between artist and audience, its "freedom of hand and thought during . . . working hours" (22:346)—for the leaden world of modern "illth," Morris foresaw with a furious conviction that the "change from old to new involves one certainty, whatever else may be doubtful, a worsening of the aspect of the country" (23:208) until "all that is old is gone, and history has become a book from which the pictures have been torn" (*Letters,* 2A:52).

In the moment that Morris saw and experienced as a knife across the retina the specific degradation of Oxford's beauty, his allegiance to the ideal of aesthetic democracy underwent a decisive change. From the first, Oxford served Morris as the benchmark in the visible Victorian world for both beauty and the sense of beauty. Any erosion of Oxford's own beauty would thus hold profound significance. To view Oxford as Morris then confronted it in November 1883 is to see that what he had long cherished as the miraculous "beauty of a town all of whose houses are beautiful" (*Works,* 23:148) had been "sold, and at a cheap price indeed: muddled away by the greed and incompetence of fools who do not know what life and pleasure mean" (23:92).

Yet the horror of Oxford's sordid subjection to the bustling shop, suburb, and tramcar reached beyond even this wounding spectacle of crassly commercial transformation to grasp the human source of its betrayal. For Oxford had been sold for a cheap price by none other than its own guardians—by precisely the university and college authorities who ought to have defended it most vigorously. "Those whose special business it is to direct the culture of the nation," Morris stormed, "have treated the beauty of Oxford as if it were a matter of no moment, as if their commercial interests might thrust it aside without any consideration." In doing this, the dons and deans of Oxford "disgraced themselves" (22:232).

When Morris returned to Oxford in November 1883, he announced his adherence to a new brotherly company: "I am one of those called Socialists" (*Works,* 23:171). On the most obvious level, this turn to socialism was dictated by Morris's implacable enmity to the economic and political order presiding over and encouraging the physical and visual degradation of Oxford, which he called Whiggery.[8] In Morris's eyes, it was wholly characteristic of the deep moral bankruptcy of Whiggery to propose to trade the incomparable and universally available beauty of Magdalen College bridge, to name just one notorious example, for the crass and class-limited convenience of tramcars and increased commercial traffic in the Oxford High Street shops.

On a deeper level, however, Morris's rebellion against Whiggery must be understood as having been dictated precisely by the Whig aesthetic tradition itself. For on its own constitutive assumptions, the Whig polity must derive its legitimacy not simply from popular consent per se but from the consent of a people known to be in communication with the realm of transcendental value. Any egregious betrayal of beauty and the human capacity for beauty, such as this exchange of the socially beneficent and historically irreplaceable beauty of Magdalen bridge for mere short-term convenience and selfish monetary gain, would call into question the legitimacy of the political order sanctioning the trade. Such a corrupt exchange would immediately suggest, in the acknowledged idiom of Whig sociopolitical discourse, that the liberal polity itself had lost its mooring in any higher idea of the *sensus communis* or common good.

Victorian Whiggery had not merely consented to but encouraged the murder of beauty and art, which Morris saw everywhere in 1883, and especially and most heartbreakingly in "this once loveliest city," as Ruskin sadly called Oxford (*Works*, 33:390). Victorian Whiggery thus had visibly resigned any pretension to communicate with the realm of transcendent value. Having abandoned this legitimating source, the liberal polity had simultaneously resigned any claim it might have once had on Morris's loyalty. In this moment Morris thus prepared to oppose and overthrow all Whiggery, turning his allegiance and hope toward "divine discontent"[9] and socialism and revolution *tout court*: "No hope save in Revolution" (*Works*, 23:92).

In November 1883, then, Morris found himself moved to a radical dissent from the atomizing and withering individualism of the Whig sociopolitical order, much as Shaftesbury had dissented from it so many years before. Where Shaftesbury, however, had half unconsciously formulated the theory of the moral-aesthetic sense to offset the destructive effects of individualist modernity on the immemorial certainties and regularities of the ontic logos and the morality of communal ties, Morris in his search for compensatory structures of human communality and solidarity set aside Shaftesburian "benevolence," refinement," and "taste." For by the second half of the nineteenth century, a morality of anti-individualism, in Michael Oakeshott's terms, had become fully available for the first time to those people who resisted the moral disposition of individualism, with its alienating insistence on personal choice, private judgment, and self-determination, quite as much as they opposed the appalling effects of chaotic industrial modernity. In this moment, Morris, who had sought since childhood to immerse himself in the richly communal life of medieval Europe through reading, dreaming, and making art, embraced the deceptively similar notions of communality and the collectivity he had located in the doctrines and practices of international socialism to resist the system that "insists on individualism and forbids co-operation."

When Morris turned to Marxian socialism, art seemed to him, in an obscene perversion of its authentic nature, the vehicle of actual social harm. In earlier years, Morris had hoped that medieval art—especially the rich tradition of Gothic handicraft—could, if its animating principle of pleasurable labor were revived, supply a model for authentic fellowship to a world riven by egoism and competition. But twenty years of trying to make that tradition bear hybrid fruit in the acrid soil of Victorian capitalism had taken their toll. Morris had already recognized the ironclad restraints—the public and business rivals without, his own artistic standards within—limiting his scope as "a would be manufacturer" (*Letters*, 2A:53). It increasingly seemed to him that a world of democracy without art might be infinitely preferable to the grinding Victorian plutocracy of art without democracy.

This is why Morris's turn to socialism produced a startling revolution in the place of art. Morris had feared and fought against the death of art and beauty all his life. Now he saw in a kind of liberating vision that there was much more to fear from the continued existence of art under the conditions enforced by Victorian capitalism than there was to dread in art's demise: "Much as I love Art and ornament, I value it chiefly as a token of the happiness of the people, and I would rather it were all swept away from the world than that the mass of the people should suffer oppression" (*Letters,* 2A:329).

If Morris could face the prospect of the imminent death of art, it was because his innate socialism and his peculiarly physical experience of beauty as somatic well-being and sensuous pleasure meant that his ideas of art already verged on the notions of material happiness, corporate solidarity, and empowerment that formed the core of the socialist agenda. Thus, he could abandon the deformed and deforming expressions of art that surrounded and oppressed him in 1883—that "hot-house atmosphere of art hopelessly at odds with the common air of day" (*Works,* 23:258–59)—while retaining what remained for him the central reality of art by preserving it under another name.

At the same time, Morris's burning conviction that a world of democracy without art was preferable to a world of art without democracy sustained itself on quite another level of experience because he had actually seen life lived without art in 1871 and 1873 when he visited Iceland. Morris's two journeys to Iceland took place during the crisis of his relations with his wife and with Rossetti, when the latter was monopolizing both Kelmscott Manor and Jane Morris. William Morris's turn to the north and to a land all but void of people has thus conventionally been seen as representing an escape from emotional complexity—from "all querulous feeling in me" (*Letters,* 1:198)—as well as a turn away from Rossetti, a man of the south.[10]

Yet Iceland also represented an anaesthetic interlude for Morris in another sense. On the outermost rim of western Europe, "in a place that looked the very end of the world" (*Letters,* 1:152), Morris found himself beyond the reach of both visual art and ordinary natural beauty. Like other artists, Morris had occasionally felt a "craving to escape sometimes to mere Nature, not only from ugliness and squalor, not only from a condition of superabundance of art, but even from a condition of art severe and well ordered, even, say, from such surroundings as the lovely simplicity of Periclean Athens" (*Works,* 23:169). But in Iceland Morris discovered how the world would look if art and beauty dropped away entirely, and in Iceland he discovered that he could bear the prospect.

This is why the Icelandic interludes represent a crucial step in Morris's progress toward socialism. For what Frederick Kirchhoff has aptly called the "zero vision" of Iceland (*William Morris,* 89) convinced Morris that art and beauty could disappear from the visible world without dying away forever. Repelled as he was by this "most strange and awful" country, "a doleful land at first with its great rubbish heaps of sand" (*Works,* 8:28), Morris came to feel in the midst of these wastes the persisting spirit of the Icelandic sagas. In his journal he marveled at "how much the present Icelanders realise the old stories" (8:45); in a letter to Charles Eliot Norton he described the Icelanders as "full of their old lore, living in their stirring past you would say, among dreams of the 'Furor Norsmanorum'" (*Letters,* 1:152).

Icelandic social arrangements suggested to Morris the form that postapocalyptic life might take. For here dwelt the material simplicity and psychic fellowship that he had been seeking ever since Oxford. Freed at last from the trammeling and "immoral" institution of domestic servants, Morris gloried in his newfound competence as a cook and his unembarrassed comradeship with his guides, who "worked no harder than we, except where their knowledge was special, and they paid us no sort of defference except that of good-fellowship" (*Letters,* 1:151–52). These rough men, living "among dreams of the 'Furor Norsmanorum,'" became in Morris's eyes the living link between the ancient "Fury of the North" (the barbarian tribes that overthrew and regenerated Rome) and the fury to come (the class rage "hidden in the breast of the Barbarism of civilization, the Proletariat" [*Works,* 23:204]) that would inevitably overthrow capitalism and regenerate the modern world.

As Morris gestured toward these "northern" virtues—"hatred of lies, scorn of riches, contempt of death, faith in the fair fame won by steadfast endurance, honourable love of women" (23:204)—he signaled his allegiance to the contemporary Teutonist school of historians. On a deeper level, however, he hailed his own political heritage as a Whig. For Morris's Iceland represents merely the latest incarnation of the "myth of northern liberty"—that appeal to the personal liberty and hardy civic virtue possessed by the Gothic tribes—cherished by Whigs in their effort to preempt the legitimacy of monarchical claims ever since Shaftesbury's friend Robert Molesworth wrote *An Account of Denmark* (1693) or James Thomson praised Laplanders in *The Seasons* (1726–30).

Yet there remains a deeper sense in which Morris's Icelandic experiences strengthened his hopes for democracy without art and the brotherly company of socialists. For Iceland's stark landscape, resembling nothing so much as "the end of the world rising out of the sea" (*Works,* 23:xvi), presented him with the visible incarnation of apocalypse, and from this idea Morris derived enormous and sustaining hope. The barren aspect of Iceland, seemingly ruined and abandoned and yet peopled with folk resistantly enduring while they harbored "the tale of the Northland of old and the undying glory of dreams" (9:125) became the visible token and promise of inevitable future change. With its grinding glaciers, seething lava flows, and "ruining streams" (9:125), Iceland seemed like a cauldron of apocalypse poised on its edge as it waited for Ragnarök—the cataclysmic final battle of northern mythology that would open the way for the return of Balder, bringing "peace and the healing of pain, and the wisdom that waiteth no more" (9:126).

This imaginative construct of apocalypse allowed Morris to master what otherwise would have been the unbearable psychic misery of art's destruction. He could subsume the death of art as a local and plot-advancing episode within a larger narrative—Marx's "providential fable," as William Dowling has called it, by which "the various modes of production generate one another in neat succession until revolution and the withering away of the state are imminently at hand" (55). Marx's acute historical analysis of the stark cleavage between medieval wealth and modern "illth" won Morris's fervent assent because it was embedded in a larger salvational plot giving him the genuine hope he needed to live without art.

Where the earlier socialist writers and preachers, as Morris declared, "based their hopes on man being taught to see the desirableness of co-operation taking the place of competition, and adopting the change voluntarily and consciously," the new school of Marx, by contrast, "starting with an historical view of what had been, and seeing that a law of evolution swayed all events in it, was able to point out to us that the evolution was still going on, and that, whether Socialism be desirable or not, it is at least inevitable." Here then, Morris stated emphatically, "was at last a hope of a different kind to any that had gone before it" (*Works,* 23:74–75).

Although Morris invoked a "law of evolution," his imagination clearly was swayed less by the ambitious claims of Darwinistic science than by the aesthetic and psychic satisfactions of romance, in which an original Edenic plenitude and harmony were lost and later regained, the romance plot assuring the inevitable outcome with the effortless smoothness of fairy curraghs on their way to Avalon. In this sense, as Jeffrey L. Spear has shrewdly pointed out, Morris was simply responding to the submerged romance plot within Marxism itself (232–33), which Morris had been reading all his life and to which his imagination now responded with a prehensile readiness.

Morris's experience of Iceland and his understanding of Marxian political apocalypse endowed him with a fund of strength, hope, and "pictures"—visual images representing substantial realities—upon which he drew for the rest of his life. Although his courage failed from time to time, so that he would feel himself "a small creature" (*Letters,* 2A:122) or "an oldish fellow" bearing "on my back a wallet of dissappointments & 'tacenda'" (*Letters,* 2A:115), Iceland, the home of the northern religion of courage, remained the site where his own physical courage was tried and proven in action.[11] Hence, it would always mark the beginning of Morris's successful effort to free himself from Rossettian paralysis and melancholy, to "look at things bigly and kindly" (*Letters*, 1:173), and to plunge into political action with "those who are in the thick of it, and trying to do something" (*Letters*, 2A:223).

In the years following 1883, Morris's hopeful trust in the socialist cause produced in him that single-minded fearlessness he had predicted of Marx's "law of evolution": "We *cant* say," he told a correspondent in 1884, "If this is the evolution of history, let it evolve itself, we won't help. The evolution will force us to help; will breed in us passionate desire for action, which will quench the dread of consequences" (*Letters*, 2A:307). Overcoming his own dread of public speaking, Morris soldiered on even across the "river of violence" (307), the "Free Speech" demonstrations in Trafalgar Square on Bloody Sunday, 13 November, 1887.

Bloody Sunday in Trafalgar Square marked a turning point in Morris's socialist crusade because it forced him to confront the vast disparity in the temporal scales assumed by Marxian sociopolitical change on one hand and by his own state of body and mind on the other. The appalling outcome of the battle between the people and the police on Bloody Sunday made clear to Morris that Marx's law of evolution would work far more slowly than he had ever imagined. Outwitted by military tacticians, unprepared for disciplined street fighting, cowed by phalanxes of mounted police and Life Guards, his socialist comrades had been stripped of all the homely symbols of their solidarity ("The band-instruments were captured, the banners and flags destroyed"), and ignominiously scattered ("there was no rallying point and no possibility of rallying, and all that the people composing our once strong column could do was to struggle into the Square as helpless units" [May Morris, 2:252]). Fought for on these terms, the "inevitable" victory of the people, Morris saw, would not come soon.

Under the differential pressure of the two time scales operating in the years after Bloody Sunday—the geological tempo of socialist transformation versus the weekly decay in his own gout-afflicted body—Morris's lifelong oscillation between ideals of art and beauty as the sign of an achieved democratic revolution and as an immediate experiential pleasure began to accelerate. Up to this point, Morris had been able to envision both art and democracy only by deferring the realization of one to the realization of the other—putting larger social ideals aside as he pursued aesthetic democracy in the specifically artistic terms of craftsmanship during the 1860s and 1870s and then putting art aside as he pursued aesthetic democracy in the terms of organized socialism during the 1880s. By the time Morris reached the 1890s, stricken in health and sunken in spirits, however, he could no longer manage the shuffle and deferral of his hopes on the old terms.

This is why the meaning of these final years from 1891 to 1896 has been so intensely disputed. For in the turn to political quietism that marks these years, from the founding of the Hammersmith Socialist Society and the Kelmscott Press in early 1891 to Morris's death in 1896, Morris's socialist partisans have wanted to see little more than a necessary period of recuperation for a man whose health had been depleted and whose spirits shaken by seven years of tumultuous and straining political struggle (see, for instance, Thompson, 582–83). Readers mistrustful of Morris's socialism, by contrast, have seen in this turn to collecting manuscripts and writing romances precisely a final rejection of those desiccating politics and a return to the genuine springs of his imaginative life (see, for instance, Tompkins, 315).

Yet if this final phase of Morris's career seems to represent on some level a withdrawal into the Palace of Art, it is because his deteriorating health compelled him to transfer into the realm of literary art the vast temporal spans necessary for sociopolitical change that now seemed to him, caught as he was within a time horizon drastically foreshortened by illness, scarcely imaginable within the domain of the real. With the socialist time scale displaced onto the enormous timescape of *News from Nowhere* and the timelessness of the prose romances, Morris could attempt to enlarge what time remained to him personally by once again experiencing "the pleasure of the eyes" on the most immediate and absorbing terms.

Imprisoned within a life shrunken by physical pain, assaulted by a degraded visual world of "eyeless vulgarity" (*Works*, 23:279) that his eyes could not shut out, Morris turned to the rich microcosms available to him within "ideal" and "painted" books. He labored at the Kelmscott Press to produce the "Ideal Book," by which he meant a book untrammeled by commercial considerations of price or audience, a book that "we can do what we like with" according to "what its nature, as a book, demands of Art" (Peterson, 67). In the same way, Morris turned to collecting "painted" books or illuminated manuscripts with an avidity contrasting strangely with his earlier frugality when underwriting socialists. For what had been the intolerable expense of money for the Socialist League and its magazine *Commonweal* in the 1880s became in the 1890s an eager effluence of blank checks poured out for medieval manuscripts. In the course of assembling what has been judged a library of "higher quality than any other major English literary figure" (Needham, 221–22), Morris spent more money on any given bestiary or medieval Bible than he ever spent in an entire year of supporting socialists.[12]

Like his old friend Edward Burne-Jones, who liked to go to the British Museum, "send for a painted book that it took a lifetime to make," and then "forget the world and live in the book for days" (Burne-Jones, 2:279), Morris regarded these books not as leisure-time toys but as harbors of refuge against the "putrid sea" of modern ugliness. "We were talking about the destruction and perishing of fine old things," as Burne-Jones later recalled, "and [Morris] said 'Well, old chap, that's one thing to be said in favour of my library—you can't drive a railway through it, eh? It's safe on that score'" (Lago, 65). Even one such painted book, the two men agreed, could reconstitute all art if ever it were swept away (Lago, 146).

Shoring his Books Beautiful against the accelerating ruin of all that ever enchanted his eyes, Morris in the 1890s thus seemed to assume the defensive but still recognizably aristocratic posture of the decadent aesthete whose yearning for cultural salvation dwindles at the end to the mere salvaging of beautiful cultural bits (Poggioli, 145)—seeds, it may be, of a possible future that would open in the cultural space beyond apocalypse. This final view of Morris as narrative poet and craftsman was proposed by as acute an interpreter of Victorian Aestheticism as Graham Hough, Morris becoming "one who keeps alive an obsolete skill, which seems hardly likely to mean much to the world he lives in, but which may nevertheless be keeping the door open for some necessary re-expansion of the artist's range, in some future that we cannot at the moment foresee" (Hough, 133).

Yet the larger significance of such a moment as this is not that Morris finally chose between his democratic hopes for art and his aristocratic responses to it but rather that the ineradicable tension between the democratic claims and the aristocratic origins within the Whig aesthetic tradition once again resurfaced into visibility. In the 1860s the democratic promise of Morris's craftsmanly ideal—that the infinitely reproducible patterns of his wallpaper, carpets, and fabrics might make available an interior world of beauty to Victorians trapped in unrelenting visual squalor—seemed at first capable of sweeping aside the aristocratic aesthetic behind Rossetti's one-of-a-kind oil paintings only to be undermined in its turn by Morris's no less aristocratic perfectionism.

Similarly during the 1890s, the promise of aesthetic democracy within Morris's prose romances was repeatedly disrupted by renegade ideological elements that resisted subordination to the utopian plot. The powerful solidarity portrayed among the various inhabitants of such an idealized polity as Burgdale in Morris's *The Roots of the Mountains* (1890), for instance, was, as a reviewer for the *Spectator* recognized, fully expressive of "the ideal sort of life that people ought to live when Socialism carries the day" (336). Yet this democratic ideal was simultaneously limited by suppressed aristocratic allegiances within the tale. For Morris's unrivaled knowledge and stubborn use in the later prose romances of the vocabulary and syntax of earlier English seemed to many of his readers not just ridiculously archaic but also to represent a linguistic gesture of exclusion, "a deliberate, and therefore self-indulgent signal," as one modern commentator has characterized this response, "that the book is for the élite only" (Talbot, 16).

"What would an ordinary novel-reader know," the *Spectator* reviewer asked, "about 'handselling' a person 'self-doom'?" (336). The author surely must have wanted to appeal to as wide an audience as possible. And yet Morris "curtails his circle very considerably by using a lingo which to many people would prove unintelligible" (335). Even a sympathetic a modern critic like Kirchhoff, whose close reading of Morris's verbal texture in the late romances reveals its larger utopian design, has concluded that Morris's archaizing syntactic and semantic structures function as "barriers [that] discourage the fainthearted and single out the 'strong of heart' capable of participating in the primitive energy of Morris's vision" (William Morris's "Anti-Books," 100). Like his fanatically "pure" and hence seemingly incomprehensible prose idiolect ("It is not written in dialect, the *Spectator* reviewer protested, "and yet requires a glossary" [336]), the interminably leisurely narrative characteristic of Morris's late prose romances tended to remove these works from the demotic reach of ordinary unleisured and unheroic readers.

Even in the most purely utopian work of the 1890s, *News from Nowhere* (1890), the ineradicable tension between the democratic claims and the aristocratic basis straining within the Whig aesthetic tradition repeatedly rises up to unsettle the placid surface of the ideal. In the privileged space of another sort of "ideal book" altogether, rising from the misty margin between the possible and the desirable, is surely, we may suppose, Morris's vision of the aesthetic state—that utopian domain where citizens will consent to the polity as unanimously and unconstrainedly as spectators of the beautiful will assent to its beauty. Freed by its fictionality from all the trammeling contradictions that enmeshed Morris's earlier attempts at ideal fellowships, *News from Nowhere* portrays the world of aesthetic democracy as a realm of unending sensuous beauty that seemingly lacks only art as such.

To enter Morris's Nowhere is immediately to find oneself in a world wholly molded by Shaftesbury's "natural moral sense." Released from all the old deforming bonds of authoritarian coercion or capitalistic contract, the citizens of Nowhere are now bound together merely "by mutual liking and affection, and everybody is free to come or go as he or she pleases" (*Works,*

16:81). The moral-aesthetic sense has become the animating principle of this unremittingly sociable world, its *sensus communis.* Without the clog of private property to hobble their natural sociability, the people of Nowhere find that the instinct for goodness—previously in the retrograde days before Nowhere confined exclusively to saints and heroes—has spread itself uniformly throughout the population. It is, as Old Hammond, the historian of Nowhere, says so ingenuously, simply easier to be good. Although there are occasional transgressions against this golden rule of good fellowship, they are, as he tells William Guest, Morris's narrator and surrogate, merely "the errors of friends, not the habitual actions of persons driven into enmity against society" (*Works,* 16:80).

Here we see the old abounding eudaemonism of the Whig political tradition—that confident equation between happiness and goodness—once more upholding and sustaining the liberal polity by means of its buoyant moral optimism. With Shaftesbury's *sensus communis* dissolving away "mere pigheadedness" in Nowhere (16:87) and inducing the minority to yield "in a friendly manner" to their more numerous colleagues (16:89), politics itself has become obsolete. Old Hammond declares proudly that he can say of Nowhere what Horrebow once said of snakes in Iceland: "We have none" (16:85). But the same thing may be said of art as such. There are, to be sure, such handsome handicrafts in Nowhere as Dick Hammond's damascened steel belt buckle and the narrator's jeweled tobacco pouch and so on. Similarly, there are pleasing bridges and houses as well as charming friezes and mosaics in the public spaces. Yet except for architecture, the fine arts have been curiously displaced. As Paul Meier has noted, both drama and music are neglected, while sculpture and painting are relatively insignificant.[13]

Even more striking, literature as such has all but ceased to be written. Indeed, the few residual traces of it, such as Boffin's antiquarian novels, are associated with the vague currents of retrogression and discontent that represent the only genuine shadow on life in Nowhere. This persistent mistrust of literature and books is symptomatic, as such commentators as Lionel Trilling, Rowland McMaster, and Barbara Gribble have argued, of a larger tension or pattern of inconsistencies operating within the work, combining to impart a dystopian dimension to Morris's socialist paradise.

The standard rejoinders to such a critique of Morris's Nowhere usually counter that any such putatively dystopian elements represent instead the critic's own bourgeois misrecognition of the condition of art in a socialist utopia. For in the perfected socialist future the aesthetic realm will no longer be divorced from the lifeworld, either by commodification or by any falsely numinous aura. Carole G. Silver has this state of affairs in mind when she says that in Nowhere "literature has [not] died. It has merely changed its form," shifting into genres that are "accessible to all, graceful, pleasant, full of incident, and appropriate in mood to their function in communal life" (121). In the same way, Stephen Coleman has argued that these ostensibly dystopian elements constitute instead evidence of Morris's realism as a social thinker, for "as a Marxist materialist, Morris was not in the business of establishing some brand of idealist perfection" (39).

Such arguments, however, fail to respond to the deeper point implicitly raised by critics troubled by the disappearance of the fine or intellectual arts within the blandly static existence of Nowhere. For their intuition of a dystopian shadow to the artless, sensuous summertime of Nowhere arises from the perception that Morris has unwittingly cut his utopia off from its essential moral source, specifically, Schiller's idea of artistic work as self-completion, which he inherited from German romanticism as mediated by Coleridge, Carlyle, and Ruskin on one side and by Marx on the other. If, as Patrick Brantlinger has observed, "experience itself is the chief art in utopia" (45), then the effortless folding of art into life, merging artistic creation with all its thought and cognitive play into a uniform sensuous experience, has at the same time silently effaced the crucial principles of resistance and cognition necessary to both art and human development as they are constituted even in utopia.

This is why critics mistrustful of Morris's Nowhere have so persistently compared its "race of fleshly perfection, worshipping phenomena, relying on appearance, arguing from sensation" (Hewlett, 350) to Tennyson's Lotos-Eaters, Morris's people seeming to inhabit the same long inertial afternoon and to harken to the same inner voice ever murmuring, "There is no joy but calm!" At times, some of the inhabitants of Nowhere even seem disquieted by their "Epoch of Rest." At the level of individual characterization, for example, Clara frets that life, as measured by the discarded old norms of nineteenth-century fiction, is no longer "interesting" enough for a novel. At the level of cultural meditation, Ellen wonders if precisely her neighbors' thoughtless contentment with their lot—"We are too happy, both individually and collectively," as one of them declares, "to trouble ourselves about what is to come hereafter" (102–3)—may not later betray them into a vacuous experimentation that will jeopardize all they have gained.

Viewed against this background of art unreflectingly lived as sensuous experience and experience lived without significant obstacle or friction, then, Nowhere has seemed to some readers to be radically lacking in the kind of resistance that Morris himself calls for in art and that Marx had posited of all genuinely liberating experience. As Morris said of his own dislike of using the typewriter and the pneumatic brush in his art, "The minute you make the executive part of the work too easy, the less thought there is in the result. And you can't have art without resistance in the material" (Sparling, 135–36).

Morris here registered in the aesthetic realm the vital importance of difficulty and opposition for provoking the deeper human creative powers to which Marx had appealed when contesting Adam Smith in the *Grundrisse:* "Smith has no inkling whatever that this overcoming of obstacles is in itself a liberating activity—and that, further, the external aims become stripped of the semblance of merely external natural urgencies, and become posited as aims which the individual himself posits—hence as self-realization, objectification of the subject, hence real freedom" (611).[14] Herbert Marcuse insisted upon the continuing necessity of negative experience, even in the Marxian utopia, in the twentieth century; for him, "It is the negative alone which is ultimately fructifying from a cultural as well as an individual point of view," because "a genuinely human existence can only be achieved through the process of negation" (Jameson, 108).

Denied this resource of fructifying negativity for evoking their own greater powers within the resistless, sensuous environment of Nowhere, the inhabitants have thus seemed to many readers finally incapable of fulfilling the utopian claims repeatedly made for them. Indeed, the inhabitants of Nowhere appear at times to constitute on the level of human activity what Morris's "force barges" and "banded workshops" represent in the sphere of mechanical operations: entities indispensable to the smooth ideological functioning of his novel but whose basis of power must finally be mystified or denied. For just as the high technological culture necessary to produce the force barges is neither evident nor acknowledged in Morris's story, so the intellectual culture necessary in some degree to artistic creation as self-realization has no admitted place amid the hay making and boat rides of Nowhere.

In this sense, Morris, who famously wrote *News from Nowhere* as a counterblast to the "Cockney paradise" pictured in Edward Bellamy's *Looking Backward* (1888), may nonetheless be seen as having produced a Cockney paradise of his own. For with its eclipse of art and intellect, Morris's Nowhere becomes precisely the utopian fulfillment of the radical Enlightenment sensualism that *Blackwood's Magazine* had long ago identified and denounced in the "Cockney school" of John Keats and Leigh Hunt. Keats's cry, "O for a Life of Sensations rather than of Thoughts!" had reverberated through two generations of Victorian poets, and Hunt's demand that "We should consider ourselves as what we really are, creatures made to enjoy more than to know" had expressed *avant la lettre* the intoxicating message of Victorian Aestheticism: "For, sweet, to feel," as Oscar Wilde declared in "Panthea," is "better than to know" (*Poetry,* 1:205).

If there was a sense in which this powerfully sensuous beauty still operated within the recognizably Whig tradition of political aesthetics, it remained a curiously limited one. Therein lay the larger significance of the narrator's reiterated praise of the Nowhere people's extraordinary physical beauty: it represented Morris's appeal to the political legitimacy of Nowhere based on precisely the grounds that had become conventional within the Whig aesthetic tradition. For just as Shaftesbury liked to point to the improved state of the arts in England after the Glorious Revolution as proof that Whig political liberty was fostering the liberal arts, so Old Hammond traced the improved state of beauty in the citizens directly to the new conditions of life in the Nowhere polity: the remarkable physical beauty of the people, he proudly tells the narrator, represented "a token of all the benefits which we have gained by our freedom" (*Works,* 16:62). Thus even though neither Morris nor anyone in Nowhere believed in a transcendent sphere beyond the sumptuous world lying immediately before them, the recognizably Whig gesture of invoking art and beauty in their transcendental relation to guarantee the legitimacy of a polity was once again ritually performed.

Yet finally even this gesture reveals the distance that intervened between Shaftesbury's Whig ideal and Morris's socialist utopia. For Shaftesbury could invoke the spreading taste for art and beauty in the post-1688 English polity as proof of its political legitimacy only because an argument could plausibly be made that the "habit of judging in the highest matters for themselves, makes [a people] freely judge of other subjects" (*Second Characters,* 23). Precisely this habit of conceptual judgment and intellectual play, of "unceasing criticism" and "boundless curiosity," as Old Hammond says so dismissively (*Works,* 16:132), has dropped out of Morris's aesthetic state.

Morris won his vision of aesthetic democracy in *News from Nowhere* only at the cost of art as such. He snatched up the wavering banner of Ruskin's Gothic ideal and restored it to a brotherly company of believers that was truly democratic, that embraced everyone, even the "grumblers." But just as Morris found in unreasoning sensuous pleasure a basis broad enough for a genuinely democratic aesthetic democracy, he turned his back on the elements that in the Whig aesthetic tradition made art specifically art as such—Shaftesbury's Platonic *to kalon,* Ruskin's Aristotelian energy of contemplation, Kant's free play of the faculties, Schiller's play-drive, Arnold's disinterestedness—in short, the critical, conceptual, and oppositional powers that combined with the liberating powers of artistic creation to transform the aesthetic dimension into a genuinely available moral source for nineteenth-century England and America.

To retain Morris's liberating, democratizing faith in sensuousness while reinstalling art at its center, then became the shared campaign of Pater and

Wilde. For as Morris himself realized, in all such battles, including the Victorian struggle for aesthetic democracy, "men fight and lose the battle, and the thing that they fought for comes about in spite of their defeat, and when it comes turns out not to be what they meant, and other men have to fight for what they meant under another name" (*Works,* 16:231–32).

IV

The Aristocracy of the Aesthetic

What is this song or picture, this engaging personality presented in life or in a book, to me? (Pater, *Studies in the History of the Renaissance*)

IF THE VICTORIAN battle for aesthetic democracy was to be fought, in William Morris's phrase, "under another name," the least likely name he would have chosen was Aestheticism. By November 1883, when Morris announced his conversion to socialism to the audience gathered at University College, Oxford, such terms as *Aestheticism, art for art's sake,* and *Culture* had become synonyms, to Morris as to all Britain and America, for the apparent betrayal of art and beauty into the hands of a self-nominated and supercilious elite. This is why Morris, even while begging his young Oxford listeners for their time and money in support of socialism, sarcastically railed at them for their "superior wisdom" and "superior refinement" (*Works,* 23:191). For as he "threatened" and "stormed at" his audience of undergraduates and dons (Quiller-Couch, 396), Morris was clearly seeking somehow to wound the insufferably languid creature beyond his grasp: the aristocratic caricature that Matthew Arnold's Oxford ideal of Culture had so inexplicably become.[1]

Nothing more dramatically exposes the tension between aristocratic and democratic impulses within Victorian Aestheticism, perhaps, than the way in which Morris's anger at such moments derived from a baffled sense of unwanted complicity. For even as he expressed his own detestation of aesthetes, Morris himself was to be nonetheless accounted "an Aesthete" by his own socialist colleagues (Olivier, 440).[2] Loathing Aestheticism, Morris was nonetheless hailed as one of its essential begetters—not only by Walter Pater, who drew the inspiration for *Studies in the History of the Renaissance* from the "aesthetic" poetry of Morris's *Earthly Paradise,* but also by Oscar Wilde, who traveled to North America to proclaim Morris as "one of the leaders of aestheticism" (*Montreal Daily Star,* 15 May 1882, printed in Mikhail, *Oscar Wilde,* 85).

In the later 1860s, when Pater first crossed the threshhold of the Whig aesthetic argument, he did so precisely as the partisan of Morris. In the midst of a gelid world of Victorian respectability and self-repression, amid a population hobbled and muffled by social and religious fears, Morris's unfettered bohemian life as a craftsman continuously presented to younger Victorians—and Pater was Morris's junior by five years—the immediate model of a fuller, freer individual existence. Yet Pater glimpsed something even more compelling in Morris. For as he reviewed three volumes of Morris's poetry in 1868, Pater saw in the shift from the feverishly dreaming medievalism of Morris's *Defence of Guenevere* (1858) to the broad daylight Hellenism of Morris's *Life and Death of Jason* (1867) and *The Earthly Paradise* (1868) the unmistakable sign of a larger cultural movement—a vital recursion to the material world of passion and sensuousness.

Morris's new poetry, Pater saw, embodied nothing less than a "law of the life of the human spirit" ("Poems," 305), the certainty that "among a people whose loss was in the life of the senses" (301) there would come, sooner or later, "a sharp rebound to the simple elementary passions—anger, desire, regret, pity, and fear—and what corresponds to them in the sensuous world" (305). Just a year earlier, Pater had written an essay portraying J. J. Winckelmann as having felt in the midst of the desiccating eighteenth century precisely what Leonardo da Vinci and Michelangelo had once felt: the "pulsation of sensuous life" in Greek art ("Winckelmann," 38). Now in the midst of a Victorian world no less frozen and inert, the unmistakable turn in Morris's poetry was signaling that the sharp rebound to sensuous life—of which the Renaissance, as Pater said, "is only a supreme instance" (305)—was gathering force in the Victorian nineteenth century.

This is why the work that sweeps up and incorporates most of Pater's two essays—*Studies in the History of the Renaissance* (1873; later published as *The Renaissance: Studies in Art and Poetry*)—demands to be seen as itself an agent of the change it heralds. Pater undertook to write a book about the Franco-Italian Renaissance, as A. Dwight Culler has adroitly phrased it, to "assist in a Victorian Renaissance—to achieve by a revival of the Renaissance what the Renaissance achieved by a revival of antiquity" (253). Beneath the aesthetic historicism of Pater's book, as his modern critics have recently begun to emphasize, there lies nothing less than "a productive program" (Williams, 65). For Pater's larger aim was to realize a dream of cultural politics: the social transformation of Victorian life through an enlarged and emboldened sensuousness—his own version of the liberal ideal of aesthetic democracy.

To understand the importance of Pater's *Renaissance* to his own generation and the later generation of Wilde thus means reconceiving that almost too familiar work as what it originally was, a political tract, a partisan document in the continuing Kulturkampf between the Whigs and the Tories, a position paper never more political than when it quietly set aside, as in the famous "Conclusion," all "political or religious enthusiasm, or the 'enthusiasm of humanity'" (*Renaissance,* 274).[3] Many Victorian readers encountering the book amid the extraordinary intellectual and social ferment of the later 1860s and 1870s became convinced that within it the current of a larger movement beat like an urgent pulse.

"Mr. Ruskin came, and the Prae-Raphaelite painters, and Mr. Swinburne, and Mr. Morris, and now lastly a critic like Mr. Pater," declared John Morley, the young editor of the liberal *Fortnightly Review* ("Mr. Pater's Essays," 476). Listing each name in this procession of the Whig aesthetic tradition, Morley portrayed each as "one more wave of the great current"[4] sweeping resistlessly against "the mechanical and graceless formalism of the modern era." Morley pointed to the "craving for the infusion of something harmonious and beautiful about the bare lines of daily living" (476) as one more sign that a larger sociopolitical transformation—perhaps even that "New-birth" through liberalism and reform that Thomas Carlyle had so bitterly derided in "Shooting Niagara" (310)—was now underway. In its own review of Pater's book two months later, the *Saturday Review,* reciting a similar roll call of artists and writers, concluded in the same heightened and prophetic accents that "all tell of a modern renaissance of the old Renaissance, of a new life sometimes surrendered to passion and to pleasure, but in its better aspects aspiring through ministration of the arts to conditions of high mental enjoyment and pure aesthetic culture" ("Review," 123).

In this heightened moment, Pater's choice of topic signaled to his Victorian readers that his affiliations and implicit agenda were ultimately political. For in choosing to write about the Renaissance, Pater undertook more than just the rebelliously anti-Ruskin gesture that his commentators have so often noted. To celebrate the Renaissance in Pater's terms was to join G. W. F. Hegel and Jacob Burckhardt in hailing its progressive and individualist character and, even more, to unite with Jules Michelet in understanding it as a specifically liberal revolution. With an unparalleled eloquence, Michelet had established the indelibly liberal character of the Renaissance, portraying it the first act of a "drama of liberty" that had culminated in the French Revolution. When Michelet's English admirers began to write of the Renaissance, they did so in the vocabulary of emancipation he had framed for them: John Addington Symonds, for one, was quick to speak of the "Liberalism of Renaissance."[5]

However unremarkable the notion of the Renaissance as a great diastolic moment of human liberation may have since become, it was identified throughout the nineteenth-century era of liberal revolutions with the cause of republicanism and reform. Invoking the Renaissance thus became during the Victorian period a recognizably political gesture with implications that were read even in such apparently neutral phrases as those Pater habitually employed. For when Pater identified the Renaissance with "liberty of the heart" and "liberty of the intellect" (*Renaissance,* 3), he grasped the idea of human freedom by superposing the Renaissance past on the Victorian present. Pater's move represents a decisive moment of temporal superposition that Fredric Jameson has portrayed as constituting "a sudden perception of an intolerable present which is at the same time, but implicitly and however dimly articulated, the glimpse of another state in the name of which the first is judged" (85).

Against this identifiably political—and politically liberal—background of the Victorian cult of Renaissance, with its "desire for a more liberal and comely way of conceiving life" (Pater, *Renaissance,* 1), such Tory critics as W. J. Courthope would trace the outlines of an ambitious "literary Liberalism." In the first three volumes of *The Renaissance in Italy* (1875–77), Courthope declared, J. A. Symonds was "quite right in identifying the movement of the Renaissance with that of the French Revolution," because both were indeed stamped with that "goal of 'self-conscious' freedom" representing the marks of both poetic Romanticism and political liberalism ("Renaissance," 21).[6] Having gained for British liberalism "a momentum of legitimacy by assimilating the march of time," as Linda Orr characterizes Michelet's portrayal of the medieval origins of the French Revolution (124), the specific political valence of Pater and Symonds's Renaissance would, upon the eventual ideological triumph of liberalism, be reabsorbed within the dominant consensus and slip from view. Earlier twentieth-century commentators would then take Victorian Aestheticism at its own estimate as deeply and "disinterestedly" apolitical, just as more recent commentators, attempting to rescue the "entire aestheticist project" from the "marginalization it has suffered at the hands of literary and cultural historians" (Freedman, 76), have gone to great lengths to display Pater's contributions to modernism and post-modernism.[7]

As a result, Pater's Victorian critics have remained, for all their vigorous antagonism and mistrust of him, perhaps his most informative. Emilia Pattison objected that Pater "writes of the Renaissance as if it were a kind of sentimental revolution" (640); F. G. Stephens wondered if Pater "goes a little too far in accepting what is called 'love'" as the vivifying power of the Renaissance (79); and Courthope denounced that "Renaissance in which the champions of 'liberal' education seek to impose on Englishmen a standard of taste that goes by the cant name of Hellenism" ("Renaissance," 30). Only in such criticism does the central place of Pater's book within the archive of mid-Victorian liberalism become genuinely visible.

To understand Pater's *Renaissance* as a document of Victorian liberalism is in turn to regard that sociopolitical formation during the period of its most vigorous ferment, the years before and after the passage of the Second Reform Bill. This is the moment in which the uniquely stimulating influence of J. S. Mill spread, under the pressure of democratizing reform, into precincts far removed from the ostensibly political. For beyond Mill's writings on representative government, parliamentary reform, or logic, his great meditation on the emergent conditions of democratic modernity—*On Liberty* (1859)—molded the moment in which Victorians first read Pater's *Renaissance.*

Convinced that these democratic conditions would oppress and stunt the powers of the extraordinary persons needed to rescue Britain from a spreading social and intellectual "stagnation" and "uniformity," in *On Liberty* Mill memorably invoked an ideal of rich individuality—an ideal nurtured, as John Burrow has characterized it, "by free exposure to 'variety of experience' and diverse modes of life, issuing in an independence of mind and spirit which Mill presents both as the goal of individual human self-development and the guarantee of future social progress" (*Whigs,* 81). This is the enormously seminal idea of *Bildung,* deriving from the Germano-Hellenic tradition of Coleridge and Schiller, Shaftesbury and Winckelmann, Pericles and Goethe—that "development of the whole complex of our sensual and spiritual powers," as Schiller called it, "in the greatest possible harmony."

Translated into specific curricular or institutional terms by such Oxford university reformers of the 1850s and 1860s as Mark Pattison and Benjamin Jowett, Mill's abstract argument for individuality and "variety not uniformity" as transformative powers capable of saving Britain from intellectual torpor and "Chinese stationariness" exerted a powerfully transformative influence.[8] "For twenty years no one at all open to serious intellectual impressions has left Oxford," Morley declared, "without having undergone the influence of Mr. Mill's teaching" ("Death," 670).

Even those who never attended Oxford or never read Mill's book came under its influence, as journalists daily translated its message into the Victorian demotic[9] and as Mill's electrifying sanction of both a rich and various individuality and a bold personal liberty against the crushing despotism of habit and the mass came to be incorporated in works barely mentioning his name such as Arnold's *Culture and Anarchy* and Pater's *Renaissance.* Mill, the younger philosopher Henry Sidgwick declared, "ruled England in the region of thought as very few men ever did: I do not expect to see anything like it again."[10]

Arnold's "Hellenism," with its stress on "criticism," "play of thought," and "spontaneity of consciousness," insinuated with irresistible gaiety Mill's critique of the Victorian cult of respectability and religion into Victorian parlors—the sanctum of that cult. This is why Morley, writing in the *Fortnightly Review* just two months before his own obituary for Mill, hailed Pater's *Renaissance* in unmistakably Millian terms as "pregnant with intellectual play and expansion" and as the "intellectual play and expansion that we require, before the social changes craved by so many can fully ripen" ("Mr. Pater's Essays," 476).

Craving himself social changes that would bring a wider liberty of the heart and of the intellect to prevail over the deadening transcendentalist cult of religion and respectability, Pater sought to portray the Renaissance as the principle of sensuous expansion and expression, constantly recurring throughout the history of the West—"It was ever taking place" (*Renaissance,* 180)—that most perfectly fulfills Mill's ideal of "human development in its richest diversity." Enclosed within this Germano-Hellenic vocabulary of self-development and enriching variety, however, resides a possibility unanticipated by Mill. This possibility is the unacknowledged yet inescapable consequence of the liberals' own appeal to Plato, to Greek studies, and to Hellenism as the best source of a civically reinvigorating power capable of rescuing Britain from the stagnation and uniformity imposed by democratic modernity—the intoxicating possibility, grasped instantly by Pater, Symonds, and Wilde, of legitimating erotic love between men (see Dowling, *Hellenism*).

It would be Pater's great distinction always to conduct his campaign for the "liberty" of the homoerotic heart and intellect from within the boundaries of the Victorian liberal discourse, especially from within the legitimating urbanity and allusiveness of the humanist tradition.[11] His constantly beckoning and receding suggestiveness in the essays of the *Renaissance* operated more as an enriching and allusive implication than as an overt appeal to homoerotic love. Yet as his first reviewers clearly suggested, Pater's unusual stress on the Renaissance as "a kind of sentimental revolution," on "what is called 'love' as the vivifying power of the Renaissance," did not escape the comprehension of his Victorian readers. They grasped on an intuitive level what Peter Allan Dale has argued constituted the twofold significance of Pater's book as, first, the mesmerizing account of "humanity's liberating movement, from the Renaissance onward, away from theism towards a 'religion' of human perfectibility," and second, the seductive vehicle for Pater's still more revolutionary "inclusion of sexual gratification within the concept of a perfect human wholeness" ("Distractions," 337).

Intent on freeing himself and his contemporaries from the brutal constraints of the Victorian cults of religion and respectability, intent on ending what he called "the crucifixion of the senses" ("Winckelmann," 48), Pater did not much consider the fuller implications of this kind of individualism—its intense and ceaselessly proliferating heterogeneity now ratified by Darwinistic science—for a liberal polity grounded ideologically in the abstract homogeneity of its citizens (*isonomia*). It had also not yet become fully clear what the new middle-class audiences for art created through Ruskin's aesthetic evangelism might do with the abundant disposable income flowing into their pockets.[12] One day not too far distant, however, the partisans of a utopian "vulgarization of art" might be forced to confront vistas of unbearable vulgarity as their audiences began to act on the aesthetic permission that had been so "democratically" bestowed.

If these disturbing developments would return to haunt literary liberalism when Wilde assumed the mantle of the Whig aesthetic tradition in the 1890s, such difficulties seemed negligible or remote in the early optimistic moments of the Victorian Renaissance of the 1870s. Pater focused instead on the revelations of Charles Darwin's science or the achievements of Morris's poetry, discovering there the buoyant assurance that what now opened to the Victorians was nothing less than Winckelmann's own opportunity—the chance "to escape from abstract theory to intuition, to the exercise of sight and touch" (Pater, "Winckelmann," 38) and to feel the pulsation of sensuous life break through the crust of the quotidian.

To make real this Victorian Renaissance, Pater proposed teaching his readers to ask the simple but revolutionary question "What, precisely what, is this to *me?* ("Notre-Dame d'Amiens," in *Miscellaneous Studies,* 117). Such Tory readers as Courthope would take this query to represent the defining question of literary liberalism, because it arose out of what the conservatives considered liberalism's central principle—the sophistical premise that "what appears true to any man is true to *him*" (Courthope, "Modern Culture," 409). When Arnold in an 1863 essay first represented Goethe as imperturbably posing this question, he meant it to express the resistance of genuinely self-responsible and enlightened thinkers to all unreflective and intransigent authority, Arnold expressing in a different register Kant's enormously liberating principle of *sapere audi,* daring to know, to learn, to become wise.[13]

When Pater repeated Goethe's question in the *Renaissance,* he shifted the stress from the individual's external relation to authority to let it fall on the individual's unique and inward experience. As noted in chapter 1, precisely this individual "liberal British soul" is ever called upon in the Whig aesthetic tradition to judge for itself. Such an ordinary "endowed soul" must therefore, as Pater suggests, learn to ask, "What is this song or picture, this engaging personality presented in life or in a book, to *me?* What effect does it really produce on me? Does it give me pleasure?" (*Renaissance,* xix–xx). At the same time, this standard of aesthetic judgment is understood as "most egalitarian" because it endows everyone with "the freedom to find on an individual basis what was most pleasing and satisfying about the work" (Court, 36).

To pose the question in this way, however, is to attack the position in Western aesthetics that, while shifting the philosophical emphasis to the subjective nature of aesthetic judgment, had traditionally denied validity to individual sensuousness. Kant himself declared that it would be "ridiculous" (*lächerlich*) for anyone to say "This object . . . is beautiful *for me.* For if it merely pleases *him,* he must not call it *beautiful*" (52). Kant rejected the formulation "beautiful *for me*" because its emphasis on private sensation denies the assumption that taste judgments are in a vital sense public—that they are subjectively universal, or true for everybody. As Paul Guyer demonstrated, Kant absorbed this assumption more or less unreflectingly from Shaftesbury and the Scottish Common Sense school, and it confronted Kant with the daunting task of providing both a working model for the operation of taste judgment and a rigorous logical proof for the claim of its subjective universality.

This enormously difficult problem was undertaken—and ostensibly solved—in Kant's *Critique of Judgment* (1790), which so massively influenced all subsequent discussions of aesthetics. Yet at the same time that Kant offered his proof of the proposition that every perceiver may be presumed to take pleasure in an object that is judged beautiful by one perceiver, he framed his explanation in language that virtually no perceiver could understand. Taste judgments are subjectively universal, in Kant's account, because aesthetic pleasure arises from the operation of capacities that all perceivers possess—namely, the harmonious free play of the higher cognitive faculties of imagination and understanding when they psychically process an object perceived under certain conditions. Kant called this process the "unification of the manifold of intuition without the use of a concept."

Just as Kant seemed to save aesthetic judgment from the unphilosophical wilderness of *de gustibus non disputandum est,* he also seemed to lose or abandon beauty to this opaque philosophical language far removed from either art as such or any actual works of art. Pater called it the "sad-coloured world of abstract philosophy" in "Poems by William Morris" (309), the world that Goethe's *Faust* had taught Pater to think of as indelibly gray—"Grau, teurer Freund, ist alle Theorie"—the realm that in the next century even philosophers would deplore for its irreducible "dreariness" (see Passmore). If the Victorians' "loss to the life of the senses" could ever be repaired, Pater recognized, all such philosophical accounts denying the aesthetic validity of the sensuous and the individual and all such language swathing actual artworks in mystifying veils of abstraction would have to be discredited. For any attempt simply to disprove this philosophical account of beauty would merely summon back and reauthorize the abstractions he wished to controvert.

To insist upon posing the question of "What, precisely what, is this to *me?*" is thus on another level of cultural implication to participate in a more profound ontological change. For Pater's defining question demands to be understood as participating in the same philosophical moment as the more famous analysis of the question, "What is that?" given in Friedrich Nietzsche's *The Will to Power* (aphorism 556, 1885–86). There, Nietzsche concluded that there is no "thing-in-itself" or "facts-in-themselves," only a multitude of interpretations projected or imposed upon those ostensible facts. The question "What is that?" thus resolves itself, Nietzsche insisted, into nothing more (or less) than "What is that for *me?*" (301).

This moment marks the end of the "world," in Luc Ferry's terms (23–24), the point of irreversible shift and acceleration in *le retrait du monde* through which the Enlightenment faith in a universal human subjectivity yields to the modernist and "postmodernist" belief in individuality *tout court*. This new sense of individuality would become so acutely specific as to be quite idiosyncratic—a *rapport à soi* intense enough, as Richard Rorty has said, that one refuses "to be exhaustively described in words which apply to anyone other than himself" (1). For Pater, no less than Nietzsche, then, the question "What is this to *me?*" marks the beginning of a deliberately "unphilosophical" project. Like the "anti-metaphysical metaphysic" of the Cyrenaic school described at length in Pater's *Marius the Epicurean* (1:128–43), the "unphilosophical" project Pater carries out within the *Renaissance* as in many of his other writings demands to be understood in philosophical terms as the continuation, by the "unphilosophical" means of fiction and belles lettres, of the democratic project found within the Common Sense tradition of Shaftesbury, George Berkeley, and Thomas Reid—philosophers whose ambition it was, as Stanley Cavell has said, "to reconcile their philosophical discoveries with the views of the vulgar" (147).[14]

Writing with his eye fixed upon the individual character understood in "its special constitution, and the peculiar circumstances of its growth, inasmuch as no one of us is 'like another, all in all'" (*Marius,* 1:143), Pater ultimately sought to rehabilitate the ground of sensuous pleasure for the individual aesthetic judgment and to do so in the name of the genuine universality that Darwinistic science had revealed to him—the universality of "man's kinship to the animal, the material," as Pater later called it (*Gaston,* 112). This is the universality that Kant's analysis of aesthetic judgment, reduced as it finally was to gesturing vaguely in the direction of the "supersensible," had so signally failed to provide.

Here, then, is the meaning of Pater's relentless, lifelong antagonism toward all philosophical abstraction and transcendentalism. This antagonism appeared in his first published essay ("Coleridge's Writings," 1866), where he insisted that any transcendentalism "that makes what is abstract more excellent than what is concrete has nothing akin to the leading philosophies of the world" (108); it continued through his fictional essay "Sebastian van Storck" (1887), with its caustic portrait of a Spinoza-besotted young man who "had come to think all definite forms of being, the warm pressure of life, the cry of nature itself, no more than a troublesome irritation of the surface of the one absolute mind" (103); and it appeared in the last work published in Pater's lifetime, *Plato and Platonism* (1893), where he repeatedly attacked the philosophical quest for the One or the Absolute as "vain," "impossible," "fanatic," and "insane."

This in turn is why Pater continually described all such transcendental ambitions in his chosen vocabulary of reproach, persistently associating transcendentalism and abstraction with words like *hard, dry, cold, freezing, inaccessible, colorless.* For example, he wrote that the idealist philosopher or "spiritualist" was "satisfied as he watches the escape of the sensuous elements from his conceptions; his interest grows, as the dyed garment bleaches in the keener air," while the artist, by contrast, "steeps his thought again and again into the fire of colour" (*Renaissance,* 177).

If Pater appears in such a passage to be raising merely "aesthetic" objections, it is because he was convinced that the aesthetic was the only possible mode of attack against the philosophical and religious hegemony that was blocking the Victorians' way to "that more liberal mode of life we have been seeking so long," a hegemony that maintained its power through forms of social terrorism. When Sebastian van Storck, for example, ignobly rejects the innocently flirtatious girl who loves him simply because he finds her coquetry "vulgar," Pater identifies this "morbid fear of vulgarity" (112) with Storck's presiding intellectual prejudice—his ruling passion for the colorless, formless, intangible world of the One. He shows that Storck's heartless rejection of the girl derives directly from the young man's first principle that "*There can be only one substance:* (corollary) it is the greatest of errors to think that the non-existent, the world of finite things seen and felt, really is" (106).

In such an episode Pater successfully portrays the ancient and inveterate philosophical prejudice against the senses, the body, the finite, and the many as a species of philosophical Grundyism—Storck obsessively pursues the colorless, odorless, intangible entities of philosophy because such abstractions are finally so respectable—and behind Pater's loathing for the Victorian cult of respectability (and the cold-blooded transcendentalism that is its philosophical voice) lies the continuous pressure of its homicidal repressions and defensive cruelties.

As long as modern philosophy simply reproduced the barren inwardness and mutilating antitheses—mind versus body, reason versus passion—of orthodox theology, Victorian civilization would find the best weapon for its own liberation rusting in its hands. As long as the question "What is beauty?" could be answered as poor, vain, plagiarizing Coleridge had answered it ("It is the unity of the manifold, the coalescence of the diverse" [Pater, "Coleridge's Writings," 123]), the power of the aesthetic to re-create social life would be locked away forever from those who most needed its re-creation. All such bloodless concepts and finespun terms were, Pater believed, not merely fantastic and unintelligible to most people; they fatally misrepresented the actual conditions of human existence, muffling those conditions in philosophically presentable veils of abstraction, in this way withdrawing men and women too far from the realities of their lives—that is, "too far from what we can see, hear, and feel" ("Coleridge's Writings," 124).

The danger was especially acute because such terms had notoriously been imported wholesale into aesthetics, and aesthetics remained, with epistemology, the one mode of philosophical analysis that still managed residually to acknowledge the validity of sensuous experience. This validity had otherwise been suppressed or stigmatized in the idealist philosophy flowing from Kant, just as it had been stigmatized and suppressed in Protestant theology. If art, as Pater asserted, "is the triumph of the senses and the emotions; and the senses and the emotions must not be cheated of their triumph after all" ("Coleridge's Writings," 124), then the first step to releasing the renovating power within aesthetic experience was to free it from the dreary spell of philosophical aesthetics.

Thus, in the preface to the *Renaissance,* Pater aggressively rejects the central ambition of traditional aesthetics, "to define beauty in the abstract, to express it in the most general terms, to find some universal formula for it" (xix). For this reason, in the vivid series of essays in "aesthetic criticism" that follow the preface, Pater works to incarnate specific manifestations of beauty in concrete works and lives from Abelard to Winckelmann, so that the phenomenon of aesthetic response would be enacted by Pater's prose speaker as a human event rather than a philosophical abstraction.

In rejecting abstraction, Pater thus specifically reverses Schiller's project in *On the Aesthetic Education of Man.* For where Schiller believed that the task of an aesthetic education was "to refer these [concrete] experiences back to those abstractions . . . to make Beauty out of a multiplicity of beautiful objects" (*On the Aesthetic Education of Man,* 113), Pater insisted that "To define beauty, not in the most abstract but in the most concrete terms possible, to find, not its universal formula, but the formula which expresses most adequately this or that special manifestation of it, is the aim of the true student of aesthetics" (*Renaissance,* xix). Indeed, for all of Pater's occasional moments of resistance to Arnold and Ruskin in the *Renaissance,* his fundamental opponent there was Schiller, who had so promisingly begun the post-Kantian aesthetic project only to congeal its liberating powers in a bewildering palaver of "insane speculative figments" (Pater, *Plato,* 31).

As usual with Pater, his contestation of a predecessor is keen but oblique, so that Schiller's presence is detectable chiefly through the metaphors the German writer bequeathed to the Victorian—"refinement," "limitation," "one-sidedness," and, most notably, "focus" or "burning point." For when Pater spoke so passionately in an earlier undergraduate essay, "Diaphaneitè" (1864) of "that fine edge of light, where the elements of our moral nature refine themselves to the burning point" (*Miscellaneous Studies,* 248) or asked in the conclusion to the *Renaissance,* "How shall we pass most swiftly from point to point, and be present always at the focus where the greatest number of vital forces unite in their purest energy?" (188), he sought to make genuinely available to Victorians the stirring but unrealized promise of Schiller's conviction that "only by concentrating the whole energy of our mind into a single focal point [*Brennpunkt,* or "focus," literally "burn point" or "burning point"], contracting our whole being into a single power, do we, as it were, lend wings to this individual power and lead it, by artificial means, far beyond the limits which Nature seems to have assigned to it" (*On the Aesthetic Education of Man,* 41).[15]

Schiller courageously decided to admit the sensuous dimension of human life to full rights with the rational, insisting that "it is the task of culture" to "do justice to both drives equally: not simply to maintain the rational against the sensuous, but the sensuous against the rational too" (*On the Aesthetic Education of Man,* 87). This bold gesture, however, had failed to survive Schiller himself. For Schiller's revolutionary message had been choked at birth by the smothering verbiage of his own prose, so that only a ghostly, idealized vestige of it remained behind to puzzle readers.

Thus, it became Pater's task to complete the "aesthetic education of man" that Schiller had begun. Pater, too, taught his readers how to "lend wings to this individual power" so that it might soar "far beyond the limits which Nature seems to have assigned to it." Now, however, these wings of transformation would be fledged from the visible world—you shall be "as the wings of a dove," promises the epigraph to the *Renaissance,* "covered with silver and with yellow gold," as the quotation from Psalms 68:13 continues—and pledged to the actual boundaries of that world.

In place of the ghostly and impalpable visions of religious and philosophical transcendentalism, then, Pater's *Renaissance* opened a vista that was frankly bounded by the iron horizon of physical death. If passion, beauty, knowledge, or a "stirring of the senses" each may offer "a lifted horizon," as the famous conclusion says, each only "seems" to do so, and even then only "for a moment" (189). Pater insisted upon the untranscendable horizon of human mortality because he was convinced that only in the shared and acknowledged condition of human materiality and finitude ("we are all under sentence of death") could men and women attain any genuine sense of their own individuality and therefore any sense of the genuine possibilities for their own freedom and sociality.

Living when disbelief in Christian immortality was spreading from circles of advanced thought to the educated middle classes, Pater sought to transform the newly reexposed horizon of human mortality from a desolating terminus into a term of emphasis that would underscore "the splendour of our experience" and "its awful brevity" (189), make poignantly apparent and precious the "work of the artist's hands, or the face of one's friend" (189), and reunite the "earthy creature" that is the individual man or woman (*Marius,* 2:223) both with humanity and with the emphatically "good, good-natured" earth (*Gaston,* 107).

In its full summons to "that more liberal mode of life we have been seeking so long," Pater's *Renaissance* exerted an extraordinary influence for so modest a volume, raising bitter opposition but no less buoyant hopes. Liberal partisans such as Symonds and Morley believed the *Renaissance* constituted a powerful new acceleration in Arnold's hopes for the aesthetic transformation of Victorian culture. They saw in Pater's sympathetic criticism—the "consideration wholly affectionate" (*Renaissance,* 48) that Pater turned upon such disregarded figures as Botticelli—the sign of "the rise among us of a learned, vigorous, and original school of criticism" (Morley, "Mr. Pater's Essays," 469). Having freed itself from the savage usages of the older dogmatic criticism (by which the Tories of *Blackwood's Magazine* had actually gloried in Keats's death), this criticism genuinely promised to become "far more helpful to the cause of general culture" (Symonds, 103).[16]

Pater's "appreciations," his "care for the lesser stars in the great firmament, his love for bits of work other than the gigantic or sublime" (Morley, "Mr. Pater's Essays," 473) projected outward as an implication of his criticism a sphere of social sympathy and reconciliation, a House Beautiful where both actual readers and figures such as Botticelli without the benefit of "a great name and authority" (*Renaissance,* 48)[17] might safely enter, just as in Schiller's aesthetic state, like "a free citizen, having equal rights with the noblest" (*On the Aesthetic Education of Man,* 219).

Inspired with the same gust of Whig prophecy that had filled Arnold when he proclaimed Hellenism as "the master-impulse even now of the life of our nation and of humanity" (*Culture and Anarchy,* in *Prose Works,* 229), Morley's optimistic prediction that Pater's *Renaissance* would help to fulfill the liberal cultural agenda to "make life more various, and to give the many different aptitudes of men an ampler chance of finding themselves" (477) swept away even Morley's own scattered reservations about Pater's book.

Yet the difficulties for liberalism raised by Pater's generous Shaftesburian assumptions—his belief in the authoritative and intensely individual aesthetic capacity of each perceiver, his confidence in each perceiver's power to seize upon passion and sensuousness without harm, his hope of a progress to human "perfection"—began to surface almost as soon as the *Renaissance* was published. The most familiar of these difficulties would be the reiterated attacks on Pater's book and on his position at Oxford by such prominent clerical and university figures as the Bishop of Oxford and the Master of Balliol, Benjamin Jowett.

The more crippling difficulty, however, always lay deeper and inhered in the textures of Pater's prose. Peter Dale has thrown a searching light on this self-divided tension in Pater's writing by stressing the profound "negativity" at the center of his work—the persistent images of death, graves, corpses. Generating an ineradicably pessimistic doubt that ever shadowed the Hegelian (and Shaftesburian) optimism of Pater's *Renaissance,* this underlying negativity tells a darker tale—"the story of the impossibility of rebirth" (Dale, "Distractions," 339), the despairing horror that no human perfection can ever arise from the grave vacated by the divine or the transcendent. Pater's negativity, Dale insists, represents nothing less than the "disintegrating core / corpse of ontology" (348), the corrupted ruin of the ontic logos when glimpsed from a position at the edge of an absconding world.

Pater's unrelenting attack on the freezing abstractions and insane speculative figments of religious and philosophical transcendentalism, coupled with his impassioned defense of the rich variety of the visible world—"It is only the roughness of the eye that makes any two persons, things, situations, seem alike" (*Renaissance,* 189)—worked in concert with the rich inheritance of Romantic poetry to make that transcendent realm seem distant and inauthentic compared to the urgently felt and sumptuously celebrated particularities of individual experience.

In Pater's *Renaissance,* one crucial element within the engine of liberal legitimation can at times be felt clashing against another, as the premise of a universal human nature required for the establishment and ideal functioning of the liberal polity (*isonomia*) begins to grind against the pluralism and individuality now required to make such a polity seem truly habitable to every "endowed soul." Twenty years earlier, Ruskin had insisted that "every man is essentially different from *every* other." Less than fifteen years earlier, Mill had declared in *On Liberty* that "the amount of eccentricity in a society has generally been proportional to the amount of genius, mental vigour and moral courage which it contained" (269). Now Pater taught a new generation to challenge the conformities and habitudes of late Victorian life by posing the question "What is this to *me?*"

As this younger generation of "singular" young men and "original" young women developed emboldened individualities through these means, they entered an aesthetic economy inflated by an abundance of new disposable income and swollen by the vast numbers of newly literate working-class audiences prepared to invoke the English right of judging for themselves. This generation became the protean and aesthetically resistant Victorian public that Oscar Wilde would confront both in the pages of *Intentions* and across the footlights during the 1890s.

When Wilde took his aesthetic message to America in 1882, he was not only prepared to assert Pater's hope for a Victorian Renaissance as an established reality but also ready to claim it in the name of his own generation. His first and most ambitious lecture—"The English Renaissance of Art"[18]—traced the history of this English Renaissance from the French revolutionaries and Keats to the Pre-Raphaelites and his own generation—young men "seeking to create a sovereignty that will still be England's when her yellow leopards have grown weary of wars" ("The English Renaissance of Art," in *Complete Works,* 10:269). Beneath the floridity of such a phrase lie the recognizable accents of Arnold, Coleridge, and Shaftesbury, as once again an inalienable sovereignty of artistic power is declared to guarantee the legitimacy of the liberal polity long after the nation's material power might have faded.[19]

His literary persona not yet fully polished, his personality not yet damaged by the invasive insolence of the press, Wilde was at his most guileless in these American lectures. The demand of the lecture format for simple formulations, his own penchant for dramatically satisfying phrases, plus the continual American encouragement to express his republican[20] and pro-Irish sentiments prompted Wilde to lay out his underlying assumptions in the baldest and most radical terms.[21] In the same way, the breathless pace of his tour would impel Wilde to borrow to the point of plagiarism from the art lectures of William Morris. This is why the essential moral optimism of the Whig aesthetic tradition came to be voiced so vividly in these American lectures and interviews, as when Wilde assured the readers of a Sacramento newspaper that the man living within "the atmosphere of fair things" must inevitably become "a better man, a better workman, a better citizen; and there will follow such a better civilization" (*Sacramento Daily Record,* 27 Mar. 1882, printed in Mikhail, *Interviews,* 68–69).

At the same time, the deep and growing tensions within the Whig aesthetic tradition first became fully visible in these lectures. Through a process intensified by the material constraints of his tour (the intrusion of reporters, the shortness of time) and by the peculiar gifts of his personality (his prodigious, "phonographic" memory [Mikhail, *Interviews,* 157], his Oxford habit of facile summation) Wilde's lectures came to operate as a medium for the free transmission of the various competing elements within the Whig aesthetic tradition—each element trailing its own ideological commitments, yet each unassimilated to the rest. In the American lectures, as Wilde spoke in Omaha, Cincinnati, and Buffalo, he thus expressed both the intense individuality and the elite separate role of the artwork and the artist—the Aestheticist themes that would so centrally concern him in the 1890s—and at the same time affirmed the democratic scope and generous utopian dimension of art, the themes that he had absorbed from the tradition of Whig aesthetics.

Here, then, was a brief moment of seeming ideological equipoise, as Wilde's "recognition of a separate realm for the artist, a consciousness of the absolute difference between the world of art and the world of real fact" ("English Renaissance," 10:256) balanced against his simultaneous recognition that "devotion to beauty and to the creation of beautiful things is the test of all great civilised nations" (10:268). The divergent assumptions about art as the world and art in the world, about the aesthetic sense as the instinct of everybody and as the gift of a few coexisted without any recognition of their ultimate antagonism. Soon, however, Wilde would be forced to choose between them.

In the years following this confident proclamation of an English Renaissance of art, Wilde's early Whig optimism began to cool. With the widening urbanization, rising standard of living, and expanding consumer capitalism of the Victorian fin de siècle, the cultural consequences of the mid-Victorian call to a noble vulgarization of art and beauty would become clearer and would suggest to many that the Whig premise of a universal aesthetic capacity had become in practice deeply problematic. As liberal partisans such as Wilde faced what appeared to be the empirical results of the Whig premise, they confronted all the oppressive visual vulgarity, the crushing ugliness of late Victorian landscapes—and especially cityscapes—now hideously defaced with the consequences of millions of individual aesthetic choices, each the result of "judging for yourself."

England had become choked with cut-rate chromolithographs, banal suburban villas, clothing and carpets shrieking with aniline dyes, an urban wilderness of advertising placards, and all the "vulgarisation" of beauty and art that the *Fortnightly Review* had so hopefully espoused in 1873; by 1880, the artist G. F. Watts told Victorians that "with regard to the eye we submit habitually to conditions which are equivalent to tearing raw meat with our fingers and teeth, living in the midst of vile odours, and complacently enduring abominable discords" (237). As conditions worsened, it seemed to many observers as if the Victorians had neither learned anything from the Aestheticist Renaissance nor forgotten anything of the pre-Aestheticist vulgarity so egregiously displayed at the Crystal Palace exhibition of 1851.

This inescapable visual degradation had in a real sense driven Ruskin mad and driven Morris, raging, into socialism, impelling both men to attack the capitalist economic order that had endowed these myriad individual choices with their enormous scope and enduring material form. This oppressive visual reality now bore down with an unendurable invasiveness upon the aesthetic sensibilities of Pater and Wilde as well, both of whom approached Ruskin and Morris in their preternatural sensitivity to visual beauty and visual blight.[22]

Yet in the end Wilde would most sharply feel the effects of the visually desolating world of democratic modernity. Thrust out of the Eden of Oxford, living by his wits as a writer and critic in the crowded and tumultuous arenas of London's new Grub Street and West End theaters, Wilde was compelled to deal with the newly democratized and vulgarized forms of art and culture on the most immediate and exasperating terms—in the form of first-night audiences, newspaper headline writers, and music-hall burlesques. What Pater, ensconced in Brasenose College, Oxford, had been content to describe as "the gaudy, perplexed light of modern life" (*Renaissance,* 182) Wilde experienced as a torsion of plastic and deforming powers.

Living in London amid what Arnold called "its unutterable external hideousness" (*Culture and Anarchy,* in *Prose Works,* 103), and thrust into a vortex of socioeconomic and ideological forces, Wilde found himself enmeshed in the machinery of the emergent culture industry that George Gissing described in *New Grub Street* (1891) with such a coruscating hatred. Wilde found himself implicated in and economically determined by the aesthetic preferences of a vast new democratic audience, its numbers swollen by working classes newly educated into "Board School ignorance" and newly endowed with leisure and money undreamt of by their predecessors. Invited by an exponentially increasing array of consumer products and impelled by the stimulus of disposable income, these audiences were now in a position forcibly to impress their aesthetic preferences on the material realm.

It was as if Pater's revolutionary question "What is this to *me?*" had somehow been turned against the literary liberals' own cultural project, now emboldening and expanding precisely the vulgarity it had once been meant to chasten and transform. For such writers as Gissing and Francis Adams, who struggled to live the life of art in grimy precincts far from Oxford, the increasing political and economic power of lower-middle- and working-class audiences constituted a bitter reminder of their own economic and social marginality. "What is that pitifulness" of the masses, Adams demanded to know, "beside the tragedy of the men of intelligence, the poets, painters, musicians?" The cry of "Exploitation!" meant little, he insisted, if it did not apply to the aristocracy of talent: "Heavens! if Labour is exploited 5 per cent., talent and genius are exploited 50 and 500" (78–79).

For Wilde, however, only slightly more insulated by his fashionable friends and Oxford double First from the grisly shambles of economic necessity, the existence of such audiences, especially middle-class audiences with their ineradicable stupidity and venomous sentimentality, projected upon the Whig premise of the *sensus communis* an unexpected and alarmingly vivid doubt. Whether he confronted them across the footlights, in the lecture hall, or from the pages of popular magazines and newspapers, Wilde realized that he faced audiences that were not simply historically new but also exerted an enormous gravitational force, remolding everything caught within its field, the arts and the artist alike.

To see Wilde struggling with these problematic consequences of the Whig aesthetic tradition is, in turn, to understand the deeper significance of the persistent deviation in his later critical essays and lectures to which Regenia Gagnier has recently drawn attention—Wilde's repeated swerve away from his announced topics of art or beauty and toward those obsessively elaborated topics of the press and the public. For as Wilde repeatedly attempted to browbeat the public into acquiescence with his own standards of taste, declaring, "Art should never try to be popular. The public should try to make itself artistic" (*The Soul of Man under Socialism,* in *The Artist as Critic,* 271), his object of remonstrance and satire began to fragment even as he lectured to it.

In *The Soul of Man under Socialism* (1890), for instance, Wilde contemned "the public," dismissing it as having been "badly brought up" (270), and excoriated "the People" whose authority "is a thing blind, deaf, hideous, grotesque, tragic, amusing, serious and obscene" (283). At the same time, Wilde paused to distinguish and honor "mankind" and "humanity"—as when, for example, he declares that a "map of the world that does not include Utopia is not worth even glancing at, for it leaves out the one country at which Humanity is always landing" (269–70). It is as if Wilde continued to recognize in "humanity" or "mankind" a residually essential ideological trace left over from the liberal past.

Finally, however, Wilde could not maintain a posture that banished "the public" in the same moment that it welcomed "mankind." For Wilde's animus against "the public" was driven by more than merely his own aesthetic distaste for the vulgarized results of reform bills and education acts. It was driven by the profound Aestheticist mistrust of all generality. Such is the larger significance of so seemingly negligent a remark as Wilde's answer to an interviewer's question early in 1895. "What is your feeling towards your audiences—towards the public?" the interviewer asked. "Which public?" Wilde immediately replied, "There are as many publics as there are personalities" (*Sketch,* 9 Jan. 1895, printed in Mikhail, *Interviews,* 1:240). Wilde's quick dismissal of the notion of a single public—and thus of a unified public sphere—represented at its deepest level a rejection of the underlying condition of possibility for such a sphere, the premise of a universal human nature.

Whenever Wilde attacked "the permanency of human nature" (*Soul,* 284), "the public," "that monstrous and ignorant thing that is called Public Opinion" (*Soul,* 275), or "that dreadful universal thing called human nature" (*The Decay of Lying,* in *The Artist as Critic,* 297), then, he was attacking the necessary basis for Shaftesbury's *sensus communis.* He was cutting the ground away from a polity that had founded—and had to found—its legitimacy and right to govern on the equal operation of its laws (*isonomia*) and the presumed universality of its citizens' capacity to choose their governors.

This danger had always resided within Pater's polemical program of praise for the rich "variety not uniformity" of the sensuous world as well as his corresponding contempt for the freezing abstractions of philosophical and religious transcendentalism. It was the danger that all universals, even those of tolerance, liberty, and equality cherished at the very heart of liberalism, would come in time to seem like arbitrary and oppressive constructs beside the infinitely various and ceaselessly proliferating particulars of actual individual experience.

Struggling to transform Victorian society through the expanded imaginative and physical powers flowing from sensuousness and individual self-realization, and portraying their opponents as devoted to freezing abstractions and vague generalities, Pater and Wilde thus found themselves caught in one of the irreducible dilemmas lying at the heart of liberalism. This antinomy of fact and theory, as Roberto Unger has termed it, arose within liberalism because liberalism, for reasons of its own ideological opposition to absolutism, rejected with one hand the realm of the ontic logos—of universals, innate ideas, and essential qualities—to which liberalism nonetheless must appeal with the other hand if it is ever to endow its own chosen arena of the empirical and the individual with any significance beyond the mere welter of discrete and incommensurable phenomena.

At this moment of ideological disarray, Wilde, urgently seeking an alternative source of moral authority for aesthetic liberalism, was moved as though by some deeper intuition to rediscover and reassert that alien principle of aristocratic spirit silently repressed by the Whig aesthetic tradition as a condition of its emergence two centuries before. The repression had never, to be sure, been altogether successful or complete, as can be seen from the charges of snobbery and vicious exclusivity earlier leveled against Arnold and Pater. Precisely the lurking suspicion of an unwarranted aristocratic superciliousness gained Arnold's essays numerous detractors in England and especially America, where even so mild an observer as Edwin Percy Whipple wondered aloud whether Arnold's "superciliousness" was not ultimately motivated by "a certain subtle, feline resentment at the non-acknowledgement of his own claims to eminence" (296, 284).

Yet Arnold, elsewhere so eloquent a spokesman for the Whig ideals of human solidarity and moral equality, was never seriously discomfited by such insinuations. Had *Culture and Anarchy* not famously declared, after all, that culture sought "to do away with classes"? The entire point of Arnold's project had been, from this perspective, "to make the best that has been thought and known in the world current everywhere; to make all men live in an atmosphere of sweetness and light." Here, in the guise of what Arnold himself would call "the *social idea*," was nothing other than the "social hypothesis" of Shaftesbury and the Stoics, granting to Arnold's men of culture, with their "passion for diffusing, for making prevail, for carrying from one end of society to the other, the best knowledge, the best ideas of their time," their determination to "divest knowledge of all that was harsh, uncouth, difficult, abstract, professional, exclusive" (*Culture and Anarchy,* in *Prose Works,* 113), the role of England's truest apostles of equality.[23]

In the same way, Pater survived with no lasting damage the bitter charge that he wrote always for an "elect," that his *Renaissance* was the rarified expression of a rarified soul, as Margaret Oliphant witheringly put it, "removed from ordinary mankind" by "ultra culture" and an entirely "academical contemplation of the world as a place chiefly occupied by other beings equally cultured and refined" (604). The liberating power of Pater's mesmerizing book, casting its spell far beyond the cultural ambit of the Oxford common room, would always be felt especially by younger readers in England and America to override such objections. Such readers found between the covers of the *Renaissance* "not a single sign," as F. G. Stephens asserted, "of more than common study or of recondite knowledge." There was only, for a generation burdened by a growing sense of the unloveliness of modern civilization, a mysteriously emancipatory experience of "delightful reading" (80).

It would thus be left to Wilde, inspired not least by the famous conclusion to the *Renaissance,* in which Pater daringly celebrated aesthetic consciousness as a last refuge from the nightmare landscape of modernity, to see that readers antagonistic toward the "elitism" of *Culture and Anarchy* or Paterian aestheticism had in their way been right all along, that an invisible ideal of aristocratic soul or spirit—Nietzsche's *seelische-vornehm,* once again—had indeed underwritten the project of aesthetic democracy from its origins in Shaftesburian moral theory. The new and potentially explosive element was Wilde's response. For if an idea of aristocratic soul was indeed inseparable from an idea of aesthetic liberalism, then those now attacking Arnold and Pater for "ultra culture" demanded to be heard precisely as the voices of a modernity not merely degraded but illiberal, an age given over, as Wilde declared, to the "heavy, cumbrous, blind, mechanical forces of Society" (*Letters,* 492) and needing nothing so much as to be confronted with a symbolic assertion of aristocratic spirit.

Wilde's later public career may be read as a virtual allegory of such symbolic assertion, especially as it involved a close relation between Wilde's own invariable pose as a dandy, the aristocrat of democracy, and such imaginary noblemen as Lord Henry Wotton in *The Picture of Dorian Gray* (1891) or Lord Goring in *An Ideal Husband* (1895). Such characters are meant to translate into an older language of rank and status Wilde's conviction that aesthetic consciousness represents, especially amid the bleakness of a modern mass or industrial society, a superior mode of existence, a way of being in the world that is in some genuine sense higher, richer, and more complete than is available to those who choose to remain ignorant of art, literature, and music. Nowhere, perhaps, are we nearer to the Shaftesburian origins of aesthetic liberalism than in the sensibility of a character like Lord Henry Wotton or in the epigrammatic brilliance of Wilde himself as he dominated London society in the triumphant years before his fall.

Wilde's aristocratic spokesmen are thus not aristocratic, his noblemen not noble, in the usual sense that denotes nothing more than a purely arbitrary superiority of heritable rank.[24] For as far as the source of superiority in Wilde's system of values is always art, the aesthetic as a timeless sphere having a power to draw the mind or consciousness of ordinary mortals toward something higher, such spokesmen express an idea of aristocratic soul or spirit still potentially universalizable. Thus, for instance, Gilbert in *The Critic as Artist* (1891) speaks not only as someone whose own consciousness has been transformed by aesthetic experience but as an apostle of the realm of art and beauty returned to ordinary existence to tell others of its wonders. Reading Homer, Gilbert tells his friend, Ernest, one does not simply read. One enters a transcendent realm of beauty where "every day the swan-like daughter of Leda comes out on the battlements, and looks down at the tide of war" (*The Artist as Critic,* 361). There, in the ideal realm of Homer's imperishable art, Helen of Troy is forever swanlike, forever "real" (362).

Timeless, universal—this vision belongs preeminently to the ontic logos, to borrow Charles Taylor's term once more, transposed from the cosmos to the realm of art and beauty. Nothing Plato ever said about metaphysics, Wilde told André Gide at this time, "could not be transferred immediately into the sphere of Art, and there find its complete fulfilment" (*Letters,* 476).[25] Yet finally even this aristocratic gesture of transcendence over the seethingly vulgar Victorian public sphere could not support the aesthete in any sustained way. For as it obeys the logic of an imperiled and transient Paterian subjectivity, Gilbert's vision of swanlike Helen is achieved only for a moment and for that moment's sake. "While you talk," the listening Ernest says to his friend, "it seems to me to be so" (362). Within the fortuitously achieved, epiphanic vision of the aesthete, swanlike Helen's "reality" can only fleetingly approach the universal cosmic order once posited by Shaftesbury's *to kalon,* that trinity of beauty, truth, and goodness understood as "the greatest realities of things," where humankind had once found the arena of its fullest becoming. So too, the ready unanimity posited in the Whig aesthetic tradition among all perceivers of the beautiful, high and low, learned and unlearned, has here been diminished to twinned souls vibrating in momentary concert.

Such a contraction occurs because, as Pater taught and Wilde's Gilbert now affirms, the world of modern thought, of Darwinian evolution, utilitarian social theory, and inexorable physical laws, has banished the idea of universals in metaphysics and morals to, a "formless and nameless infinite world" (Pater, "Sebastian Van Storck," 110), the graveyard of those unreal abstractions that earlier civilizations had deluded themselves into mistaking for reality. "The world through which the Academic philosopher becomes 'the spectator of all time and of all existence,'" Gilbert warns Ernest, "is not really an ideal world, but simply a world of abstract ideas. When we enter it, we starve amidst the chill mathematics of thought" (381). Compared to the "finite world of what is seen and felt," where the individual "endowed soul" realizes itself in the fullest intensity of its subjectivity, Shaftesbury's *to kalon* had become for liberal Aestheticism an alienating, uninhabitable realm—no longer the greatest reality but merely the "dry and seedy and wooden" husk of a life (Pater, *Plato,* 159) that can be authentically lived, which is to say, lived "intensely, fully, perfectly" (Wilde, *Soul,* 288), only somewhere beyond the freezing circumference of the universal.

The notion of an aesthetic elect, an aristocracy of mind or spirit dwelling among the teeming masses of the modern age, arises in this situation because art, no matter how timeless or transcendent, cannot by its mere existence hold out any promise of salvation. One must, in short, accept the gift of inward transformation that comes from gazing upon the Mona Lisa with eyes that can see her eternal mystery or watching swanlike Helen appear high upon the walls of Troy. But most souls in the clamorous world of modern industrial democracy have shown no desire to do so. The moral emphasis of aesthetic liberalism thus shifts in the moment of its extremity, as the title of Wilde's *The Critic as Artist* is meant to insist, from art and beauty as such to salvation through aesthetic response: the realm of *to kalon* is no longer some eternal order of the universe but an order of intersubjective experience mysteriously sustained by an art that exists outside the flux of things.

Wilde still possessed a social vision—he would not otherwise have written a work such as *The Critic as Artist* to convince others of the transcendent value of art—but his vision was haunted by an uneasy sense that aesthetic democracy may have been, after all, nothing more than a pleasing delusion or dream. For even as aesthetic liberalism managed for one extended cultural moment to find in Wilde's writings the saving possibility of its survival among a fugitive elect, it was compelled to confront the squalid reality of an age and society—and the equally grim forces of impersonal historical process—that imperiled its existence as a system of values. To see how often Wilde was compelled to speak as though to an aristocracy of scattered spirits raised by art and timeless beauty above the swarming vulgarity of the age is inescapably and simultaneously to see that such an elite, like an earlier European aristocracy based on birth and privilege, was very likely a remnant on its way to extinction.

Wilde's own tendency to see himself as an aristocratic soul or spirit doomed to linger on into a shrunken age explains not only his strong personal identification with the wits and rakes of the Restoration and early eighteenth century—he was, said Yeats, "one of our eighteenth-century duellists born in the wrong century" (*Memoirs,* 22)—but also a certain quality of sheer recklessness that marked his actions after his early rise to fame. For what in retrospect is likely to look merely like hubris, the unreflective egoism of someone who had achieved celebrity too soon, was in the period of happy innocence before Wilde's fall something else entirely, an actual belief in the power of art—Shaftesbury's *to kalon* as that transcendent realm in which beauty and virtue were quite literally inseparable—to exempt its devotees from bourgeois morality. True culture, declares Gilbert in *The Critic as Artist,* nowhere more purely Wilde's spokesman than here, makes sin impossible to the "elect," even should such chosen souls indulge in "acts or passions that with the common would be commonplace, or with the uneducated ignoble or with the shameful vile" (*The Artist as Critic,* 406–7).

When Wilde was arrested and put on trial in the spring 1895, it was as much for sentiments like this as for his behavior, thus demonstrating the degree to which, as Wilde stepped into the prisoner's dock, aesthetic liberalism was on trial as well. Although his own sense of belonging to an aesthetic elect had led Wilde to engage in such perilous public acts as entertaining male prostitutes at the Café Royal and consorting with the beautiful but forbidden son of the marquess of Queensberry, the Crown would introduce as evidence against him not simply indications of the "gross indecency" it was ostensibly prosecuting but such works as *The Picture of Dorian Gray* and "Phrases and Philosophies for the Use of the Young."[26] In these writings, the aesthete's creed had been laid out as though in cool and deliberate disdain for bourgeois morality. The sense in which this was a symbolic assertion of aristocratic soul or spirit was not lost on the onlookers. "Here are some *more* aristocrats!" howled the crowds greeting the arrival of Wilde's friends at his final criminal trial. "Here are some more of them!" (Sherard, 187; emphasis added).

The harrowing and pitiable spectacle of Wilde's trials in the spring 1895 must be understood in this context, not simply as a rupture within liberal culture but as a ritual in which Wilde himself was cast in the role of *pharmakos* or scapegoat in relation to a liberalism that had at long last grasped the pointlessness of trying to claim for itself any grounding in transcendent values. Previously, the Tory opponents of popular consent had argued that the liberty proclaimed so paramount a good by Whig or liberal theory was in its very nature inseparable from license or licentiousness, that in a society cut adrift from divine justice or natural law the only measure of right and wrong would speedily approach that rule of mindless hedonism denounced by Arnold under the name of doing as one liked. Yet the body that prosecuted Wilde for sodomic indecency in 1895 was not these clamorous Tory foes of license and licentiousness but the Liberal government of William Ewart Gladstone and the earl of Rosebery.[27]

The significance of the Wilde episode as a symbolic drama of sacrifice and redemption has always at some level been understood to derive from Wilde's own paradoxical status as a figure at once marginal and central to late Victorian culture; Jonathan Dollimore has recently characterized Wilde's marginality, as "always interior to, or at least intimate with, the center" (37). The explanation of Wilde's centrality, to anyone familiar with the Whig aesthetic tradition, also is not hard to see: from Shaftesbury and his eighteenth-century followers to Ruskin, Morris, and Pater, the idea of *to kalon* had never lost its promise as a potential source of legitimation for the liberal polity. Even amid the ironies and hesitations of *The Soul of Man under Socialism* lies the lingering power of Shaftesbury's idea of the *sensus communis*.

Nothing so poignantly signals the degree to which the *sensus communis* had by Wilde's day been exposed as an empty dream, on the other hand, than his own isolation as an aristocrat of aesthetic consciousness doomed to dwell in a low and shrunken age. For this isolation not only gives us the sense in which Wilde's noble or aristocratic bearing had always been, even in the years before his fall, an unsuspected measure of his marginality but also in which the vision of *to kalon* had some time since ceased to bear any functional relation to the ideology of the liberal state. What is sacrificed in symbolic terms when Wilde is "swept down" the courtroom stairs leading to "the bottomless pit" of imprisonment and shameful exile (Sherard, 191) is not simply the vision of *to kalon* and the doctrine of the *sensus communis* but also the very pretense that, under the arrangements of modern democracy, the state needs any source of legitimation other than that provided by popular opinion.

A ritual of purification could be played out on such terms in the 1890s no doubt because of the newness of the idea that popular opinion might be a sufficient ground of legitimation for the liberal polity—the sort of "antifoundational" notion of legitimacy subsequently articulated by John Dewey and still being urged in our own day by philosophers like Richard Rorty. Simultaneously, there arose a troubled awareness that, from the gods of the Greeks and Romans to the divine right of European monarchy, no society in history had been able to imagine itself except as grounded in some order of transcendental value external to human contingency. At any rate, this logic seems powerfully to cast Wilde at the moment of his tribulation in the role of *pharmakos,* the sacrificial victim described by René Girard in *Violence and the Sacred* as having symbolic value precisely as he occupies a problematic situation between the inside and the outside, somehow belonging at once "to both the interior and the exterior of the community" (272).

In Girard's theory of regenerative violence, however, as in Christian theology and a line of anthropological speculation going back to James Frazer's *Golden Bough,* the symbolic victim is to draw down upon himself all the free-floating dissension scattered throughout the larger community. As a result, with the single stroke of ritual sacrifice some ground of otherwise intolerable contradiction is eliminated and the social equilibrium is restored. In the Wilde episode, which marked not some archetypal moment of communal origins but a moment of rupture and reestablishment within an ongoing culture, the same logic of symbolic sacrifice is to a degree obscured by a cluttered surface of public events and sensational details, and yet its mythic outlines have always been more or less apparent. In the condemnation of Wilde, amid the ancient legal panoply of gowns, wigs, and warders, one still glimpses the symbolic ritual through which a liberal political order, able in this highly charged atmosphere to exercise authority even while giving up any claim to legitimacy beyond customary law and popular opinion, has begun at last to function in wholly modern terms.

The project of aesthetic democracy in some formal sense came to a conclusion with Wilde's removal to Holloway prison, but its last real appearance in the public domain came, amid tragicomic circumstances, in the earlier courtroom exchanges in which Wilde had been hounded by the prosecutors about his unlikely preference for the company of lower-class boys. What else but the prospect of gross indecency with another male person, Wilde was asked again and again, could explain why an Oxford honors graduate and celebrated author, a famous aesthete in all the perfumed perfection of his fastidious role, would seek out the company of telegraph boys and grooms? To which Wilde's answer, sustained with a dignity that even in these unlikely circumstances suggested some deeper consistency of belief, was always some variation on the theme: "I make no social distinctions"; "I didn't care twopence what they were. . . . I have a passion to civilize the community" (Hyde, 316, 143).

To hear in such replies the desperate inventiveness of a brilliant mind driven back upon the last resources of self-vindication is, no doubt, to hear most of what matters in Wilde's utterance. Yet there remains the question of why, at this moment of extremity, he chose to justify himself in these rather than any other terms. The answer is that Wilde was giving voice to a doctrine to which, in better times, he had devoted his life and his talent, an actual belief in the power of art to civilize the community, to create in the modern age a world without social distinctions—the credo, in short, of aesthetic democracy, going back through Morris, Ruskin, and Schiller to the third earl of Shaftesbury. In the originary moment of the liberal or Whig tradition, Wilde attempted to discover in the vision of *to kalon* and the *sensus communis* a basis of human community that might be at once just and harmonious, purposeful and free.

Notes

Works Cited

Index

Notes

I. Victorian Liberalism and Aesthetic Democracy

1. This new, recognizably Habermasian Shaftesbury has reappeared in Lawrence Klein's *Shaftesbury and the Culture of Politeness,* a work published too late for full consideration here. Although considerably overestimating Shaftesbury's pursuit of modernity, autonomy, Ciceronianism, and "discursive liberty," Klein valuably stresses the ideological role of *Characteristics* in legitimating the post-1688 Whig political order.
2. Here and in subsequent quoted passages I have silently modernized earlier orthography and punctuation.
3. Although *Two Treatises* was published anonymously in 1690, Peter Laslett has determined that within two years James Tyrell knew of Locke's authorship and many other readers, both in England and on the Continent, suspected it.
4. See John Dunn for evidence that by "consent" Locke is referring to the origin of legitimate societies, not to their mode of political organization. As Quentin Skinner and others have noted, there is always a danger of attributing to Locke himself the liberal political notions that he would simply make possible. The account of Locke given here focuses on the way Shaftesbury and later figures understood him, reading within the tradition of political liberalism. Shaftesbury himself ever strove to disguise his deep philosophical differences with Locke, warning a correspondent in a private letter of 1709—five years after Locke's death—"Thus have I ventured to make you the greatest confidence in the world, which is that of my philosophy, even against my old tutor and governor, whose name is so established in the world, but with whom I ever concealed my differences as much as possible" (*Life,* 416).
5. For a somewhat different account of Shaftesbury's moral-aesthetic theory as legitimizing the Whigs' "transition from an aristocratic dominion based on agriculture to an oligarchic dominion based on agriculture and commerce" see Caygill, 50.
6. Cf. Shaftesbury, *Second Characters:* "An ingenious author and notable metaphysician [i.e., Locke] about twenty years ago took such an advantage from the affected fulsome and common use of instinct and innate ideas, that being extremely well received and heard on account of his excellent genius and capacity in other writings, these words grew so out of fashion that a man of sense durst hardly use them on the most proper and obvious occasion. And it was safer for a gentleman who was a lover of sports to say seriously upon the subject of his chase, that his dog, jowler, or tomboy reasoned or meditated, than that he had *natural sagacity* or *instinct*" (106). See also *Life,* 414–15.
7. Laslett discusses the 1690 letter from Locke's friend, James Tyrell, informing Locke that "some thinking men at Oxford" were "dissatisfied with what you have said

concerning the law of nature (or reason) whereby we distinguish moral good, from evil and virtue from vice" (79–82). Locke's phrase "writ in the hearts of all mankind" employs the language of Paul's "law . . . written on their [i.e., the Gentiles'] hearts" in Romans 2:15 to express Cicero's idea of natural law: "Est quidem vera lex recta ratio, naturae congruens, diffusa in omnes, constans, sempiterna" (*De Re Publica,* 3:22).

8. Arising at the time of the Reformation, the identification of the partisans of liberty with libertines or advocates of moral and especially sexual license had become a standard mode of attack among the English defenders of religious and political tradition, later to be known as Tories. Locke is responding to this polemical move in the second treatise by anticipating it when he says of the Whig polity, "But though this be a state of liberty, yet it is not a state of license" (2:270).

   Shaftesbury, declaring that the defense of moral and political liberty was "the hinge and bottom" of *Characteristics* (*Life,* 449), remained acutely aware that the Tories would take any opportunity, as he said, to "confound licentiousness in morals with liberty in thought and action" (*Characteristics,* 2:346). At the same time, Shaftesbury was aware, as he noted in his journal, that "liberty of thought and writing will produce a sort of libertinism in philosophy, *which we must bear with*" (*Life,* 353; emphasis added).

   It remains one of the more poignant ironies of cultural history that even Shaftesbury's most devoted disciple, Francis Hutcheson, was forced to concede that some men at least took his "libertinism in philosophy" for libertinism *tout court:* "How would it have moved the indignation of that ingenious nobleman, to have found a dissolute set of men, who relish nothing in life but the lowest and most sordid pleasures, searching into his writing for those insinuations against Christianity, that they might be the less restrained from their debaucheries; when at the same time their low minds are incapable of relishing those noble sentiments of virtue and honor, which he has placed in so lovely a light!" (xxi–xxii).

   Gertrude Himmelfarb has noted that the word *license* nowhere appears in the great charter of nineteenth-century liberalism, J. S. Mill's *On Liberty,* "perhaps because it suggests that there can be an excess of liberty" (534).

9. Robert Voitle notes that Shaftesbury added the aesthetic analogy to the 1711 version of the *Inquiry Concerning Virtue or Merit* published in *Characteristics;* by contrast, in the 1699 version of the *Inquiry,* Shaftesbury had referred only to the moral sense. Ernest Tuveson traces the source of the analogy to Thomas Burnet, a disciple of the Cambridge Platonists, who had asserted in an anti-Locke pamphlet of 1697, "This I am sure of, that the distinction, suppose of gratitude and ingratitude, fidelity and infidelity, . . . and such others, is as sudden without any ratiocination, and as sensible and piercing, as the difference I feel from the scent of a rose, and of assa-foetida" (243). Jerome Stolnitz has stressed the "devious" and M. H. Abrams the "accidental" character of the subsequent elaboration of philosophical aesthetics from Shaftesbury's analogy.

10. Shaftesbury expressed his confidence in the taste of ordinary people throughout *Second Characters.* See, for instance, the jotted notes of p. 177: "The philosopher and virtuoso alone capable to *prove, demonstrate* [the rules of morals and the rules of perspective]. But the idiot [i.e., "one not professionally learned or skilled"], the vulgar man *can feel, recognise.* The eye has [a] sense of its own, a practiced method

peculiar and distinct from common reason or argumentation" (emphasis added). It would even appear that Shaftesbury empirically tested the capacity for aesthetic response in at least one untrained perceiver, reporting that "an innocent child's eye (of good parts and not spoilt already by pictures of the common sort) always found the best, as I have found experimentally in such a one not of the higher gentry but liberal, and out of the way of prints, and such costly playthings of imagery, etc. The same experienced as to likeness in portraiture" (115–16). Claims put forward in recent years by John Barrell, Robert Markley, Ronald Paulson, and others regarding the elitist or exclusivist character of Shaftesbury's aesthetic theories cannot be sustained by a reading of the full range of his writings.

11. Cf. also this passage by Shaftesbury's influential disciple, William Melmoth: "The charms of the fine arts are, indeed, literally derived from the author of all nature, and founded in the original frame and constitution of the human mind. Accordingly the general principles of *taste* are common to our whole species, and arise from that internal sense of beauty which every man, in some degree at least, evidently possesses. . . . The truth is, taste is nothing more than this universal sense of beauty, rendered more exquisite by genius, and more correct by cultivation" (2:110–11). A. O. Lovejoy notes that Melmoth's *Letters* (1749) went through at least twelve London and three American editions (295n). Even James Usher, who declared himself at all other points an opponent of Shaftesbury's doctrines, conceded that real taste is the property of all men, "the savage and courtier, the rustic and philosopher, the Indian and European" (34–35).
12. In these notes Shaftesbury urged himself to abandon the rhapsodic mode of *The Moralists* and in the new work (to be known as *Second Characters*) to return to the lighter, epistolary style he had adopted in the *Miscellanies* section of *Characteristics.* Shaftesbury repeatedly told himself to disguise from his readers the real ethical purpose of the book: "To twist, as it were, and interweave morality with plastics [i.e., remarks on the visual arts], that supreme beauty with this subaltern" (9). In this way, the "secret anti-Epicurean view running through the whole" of *Second Characters* will be imparted "darkly or pleasantly with raillery upon self; or some such indirect way" (6) to readers who might otherwise resist his moral counsel. Those modern critics of Shaftesbury who habitually ignore the *Regimen* and *Second Characters* are repeatedly misled by the similarly disguised purposes of the *Characteristics,* mistaking Shaftesbury's attempt to salvage by means of philosophy and the arts a vacuous, potentially corruptible, and hence dangerous class of patrician young men for what is asserted to be a hegemonic defense of aristocratic privilege.
13. Quoted from apRoberts, who notes that Matthew Arnold copied this same passage from Burnet into his notebook during the late 1860s (146).
14. See, for example, James Arbuckle: "I have seen the Lord Shaftesbury's works on a shopkeeper's counter, and hear him every day quoted by persons, whose business it neither is to understand him, nor have they proper means of doing it; and who when they have got a little smattering of him, for the most part employ it to very ill purposes" (2:227).
15. For an analysis of Winckelmann detailing his debt to the English tradition of classical republicanism, e.g., his wholesale transcription of passages from Trenchard and Gordon as well as from Shaftesbury into his commonplace book, see Chytry, 27. For Shaftesbury's influence on Schiller, see Carter and Cassirer.

16. R. G. Collingwood pointed out many years ago that "as the Greeks have no word for art, so they have no word for beauty" (162). In Plato's *Republic,* he continues, "the specialised and isolated form of aesthetic experience which we call *par excellence* the life of art is certainly by him excluded from the ideal state, as being no true element in the life of reason; but aesthetic experience as such remains for him a permanent and necessary part of the life of reason, in so far as that experience is modified or controlled by reason itself." Collingwood clarifies this point by saying, "Art is not banished from the ideal state. It remains the great educative power by which the young guardians are to be trained; and even the mature guardians are to continue in the practice of it, in shapes suitable to their intellectual and moral stature" (164).

    Paul Oskar Kristeller's notable essay, "The Modern System of the Arts," provides the classic account of the eighteenth-century invention of the "fine" arts: "We have to admit the conclusion, distasteful to many historians of aesthetics but grudgingly admitted by most of them, that ancient writers and thinkers, though confronted with excellent works of art and quite susceptible to their charm, were neither able to nor eager to detach the aesthetic quality of these works of art from their intellectual, moral, religious and practical function or content, or to use such an aesthetic quality as a standard for grouping the fine arts together or for making them the subject of a comprehensive philosophical interpretation" (174).
17. See Schiller, *Aesthetic Education:* "Beauty alone can confer upon [man] a social character. Taste alone brings harmony into society, because it fosters harmony in the individual. All other forms of perception divide man, because they are founded exclusively either upon the sensuous or upon the spiritual part of his being; only the aesthetic mode of perception [*die schöne Vorstellung*] makes of him a whole, because both his natures must be in harmony if he is to achieve it. All other forms of communication divide society, because they relate exclusively either to the private receptivity or to the private proficiency of its individual members, hence to that which distinguishes man from man; only the aesthetic mode of communication [*die schöne Mitteilung*] unites society, because it relates to that which is common to all [*auf das Gemeinsame aller*]" (215).
18. See Kant's "Third Critique": "I say that taste can with more justice be called a *sensus communis* than can sound understanding; and that the aesthetic, rather than the intellectual, judgement can bear the name of a public sense" (153). In a valuable analysis of Kant's aesthetic theory, Paul Guyer has characterized such remarks as the unassimilatable residue left over from Kant's early and Shaftesburian commitment to communicability as the ground of taste in the *Logik Blomberg* (1770). There Kant declared, "In everything pertaining to taste, a sociability is the ground and therefore elevates taste much; he, who merely chooses what pleases himself but no one else, has indeed no taste. It is therefore impossible for taste to be isolated and private. Judgment about taste is therefore never a private judgment" (Guyer, 25). For Shaftesbury's influence on Kant, see also Dunham and Carritt.

II. Ruskin's Law in Art

1. For the role of Dr. Henry Acland and the cholera epidemics of the 1850s in the founding of the Oxford museum, see Hilton, 216–25.

2. For a provocative analysis of the 1851 exhibition arguing that "far from being an actual cornucopia, the Crystal Palace was an extraordinary collective bluff" that "actually helped to create the sense of surplus that it is so often cited as evidence for," see Richards, 17–72.
3. Shaftesbury's emphasis on disinterestedness and sociability reached Arnold and Ruskin through the works of Joseph Butler (1692–1752), whose *Rolls Sermons* (1726) and *Analogy of Religion* (1736) had become set texts in the Oxford *Literae humaniores* school following Coplestone's curricular reform of 1800. For Shaftesbury's specific influence on Butler, see Sidgwick, 190–98. For Arnold's bemused meditation on Butler, who had been disestablished from the Oxford Greats curriculum following a second set of reforms in 1850, see his 1876 essay "Bishop Butler and the Zeit-Geist," *Prose Works,* 8:11–62.
4. This is the deeper explanation, one suspects, for the oddity in Ruskin's terminology for Venetian architectural ornament to which A. D. Culler has recently called attention: "It is odd," Culler says, "that Ruskin should use the term *Constitutional,* which is an eighteenth- and nineteenth-century term of Whig political theory, to describe the ornament of the Middle Ages. *Feudal* would have been more exact" (169). But Ruskin calls his ideal architectural mode "constitutional" precisely to stress the reciprocity between sociopolitical conditions and artistic achievement that Shaftesbury had emphasized in his letter to Lord Somers—an assumption about political liberties and aesthetic freedom that had become in the years following the publication of the *Characteristics* such a commonplace that even Shaftesbury's opponents did not hesitate to agree with him about it. James Usher, for instance, who considered Shaftesbury and Hobbes equally reprehensible as "patrons of licentiousness" (98), declared in 1769, "The fine arts only arrived to perfection in free countries, because liberty is the very soul, and inspiriting idea of the arts" (206).

   For this reason, Ruskin's somber meditation in *Stones of Venice* on the causes of national greatness and decline—England's decline as well as Venice's—demands to be read in the context of the pervasive Old Whig, Country-party, and Opposition fears of "corruption" and national "ruin" during the eighteenth century. Ruskin's essentially civic elegy on the decayed republic of Venice derives in direct ideological terms from James Thomson's *Liberty* (1735–36), in which the goddess Liberty declares of Venice, "To this fair Queen of Adria's stormy gulf, / The Mart of Nations! long, obedient seas / Rolled all the treasure of the radiant East. / But now no more."
5. Although seeming to change his mind later on, Ruskin at first vociferously refused to use the relatively new English word *aesthetic* (which had been introduced by Carlyle and come into use among Germanophile undergraduates at Oxford during the 1840s; see Carr; Scott), which Ruskin considered to be "that pigs' flavouring of pigs'-wash," as he called it in 1881 (*Works,* 4:xlviii). To Ruskin's etymologically attuned ear the Greek *aisthēsis* emphasized the physical response over the contemplative experience he believed to constitute the perception of the beautiful. Ruskin seemingly was never able to find a semantic path between what he loathed as the sensual and what he clung to as the theoretic or contemplative, because he habitually used *sensual* where *sensuous* might have served.
6. When Ruskin reissued *Modern Painters* in 1883, he noted of this passage concerning "energy of Contemplation" from volume 2, "It seems to me now amazing that I acknowledge no indebtedness to this passage [from Aristotle's *Ethics*] and its context,

which seem, looking from this distance of years, to have suggested the whole idea of my own essay" (*Works,* 4:145n). See also Gilbert. Similarly, Ruskin thought better of his remark deprecating all pursuits that have any "taint in them of subserviency to life" by declaring, "'Taint' is a false word. The entire system of useful and contemplative knowledge is one; equally pure and holy: its only 'taints' are in pride, and subservience to avarice or destruction" (4:35n).

7. See, for example, the appendix on modern education in volume 3, where Ruskin declared, "*Every* man is essentially different from *every* other, so that no training, no forming, nor informing, will ever make two persons alike in thought or in power. Among all men, whether of the upper or lower orders, the differences are eternal and irreconcilable, between one individual and another, born under absolutely the same circumstances. One man is made of agate, another of oak; one of slate, another of clay. The education of the first is polishing; of the second, seasoning; of the third, rending; of the fourth, moulding. It is of no use to season the agate; it is vain to try to polish the slate; but both are fitted, by the qualities they possess, for services in which they may be honoured" (*Works,* 11:262).

   Ruskin's preaching was not at odds with his practice as an art teacher in the Working Men's College (1854–58). One of his students recalled, "How generous he was! He taught each of us separately, studying the capacities of each student. For one pupil he would put a cairngorm pebble or fluor-spar into a tumbler of water, and set him to trace their tangled veins of crimson and amethyst. For another he would bring lichen and fungi from Anerley Woods" (quoted in Hilton, 204).

8. For example, Unrau stated that Ruskin's notion that imperfect Gothic hands produced unassailable Gothic wholes "has proven, for many readers, an attractive notion; but it bears little relation to the truth. The probable response of a Gothic master mason to Ruskin's proposal that 'any degree of unskilfulness should be admitted, so only that the labourer's mind had room for expression' is concisely indicated in the following article from a medieval code of masonry: Yf hit befall th[t] any mason th[t] be perfyte and connyng come for to seche werke and fynde any vnperfit and vnkunnying worchyng the master of the place shall receyue the perfite and do a wey with the vnperfite to the profite of his lord'" (39).

9. See Ruskin, *Stones of Venice,* vol. 1: "I set myself, therefore, to establish such a law, in full belief that men are intended, without excessive difficulty, and by use of their general common sense, to know good things [in architecture] from bad" (*Works,* 9:56). For Ruskin's familiarity with the Scottish moral sympathy or Common Sense philosophers, see Landow, *Aesthetic and Critical Theories,* 95–96, 154, 353–54. Jeffrey L. Spear notes that Ruskin's mother was reading Adam Smith's *Theory of the Moral Sentiments* (1759) to him at the age of ten (156). For the distinctively Scottish emphasis on "civil society," see Burrow, 211–49. Compare also the following two passages from Ferguson's *An Essay on the History of Civil Society* (1767) and from Carlyle's "Characteristics" (1831): "The experience of society brings every passion of the human mind upon its side. Its triumphs and prosperities, its calamities and distresses, bring a variety and a force of emotion, which can only have place in the company of our fellow-creatures. It is here that a man is made to forget his weakness, his cares of safety, and his subsistence; and to act from those passions which make him discover his force" (Ferguson, 18); "It is in Society that man first feels what he is; first

becomes what he can be" (Carlyle, "Characteristics," 28:10). Carlyle's title "Characteristics" alludes to Shaftesbury (see Carlyle, *Collected Letters,* 1:50–51), whose work Carlyle had read in 1826.

10. In *Seven Lamps of Architecture* Ruskin attacked liberty in these terms: "How false is the conception, how frantic the pursuit, of that treacherous phantom which men call Liberty: most treacherous, indeed, of all phantoms, for the feeblest ray of unreason might surely show us, that not only its attainment, but its being was impossible. There is no such thing in the universe. There can never be" (*Works,* 8:248–49). In *Unto This Last* he declared, "If there is any one point insisted on throughout my works more frequently than another, that one point is the impossibility of equality" (*Works,* 7: 00). And in *A Joy Forever* he remarked of the various French attempts at fraternity, "They got all wrong in their experiments, because they quite forgot that this fact of fraternity implied another fact quite as important—that of paternity, or fatherhood. That is to say, if they were to regard the nation as one family, the condition of unity in that family consisted no less in their having a head, or a father, than in their being faithful and affectionate members, or brothers" (16:24).
11. Even as late as 1870, in the first of his lectures as Slade Professor of Art at Oxford, Ruskin declared, "There is no limit to the good which may be effected by rightly taking advantage of the powers we now possess of placing good and lovely art within the reach of the poorest classes." At the same time, however, he had come to see that this noble vulgarization of art brought with it inescapable dangers: "First, by forms of art definitely addressed to depraved tastes; and, secondly, in a more subtle way, by really beautiful and useful engravings which are yet not good enough to retain their influence on the public mind;—which weary it by redundant quantity of monotonous average excellence, and diminish or destroy its power of accurate attention to work of a higher order" (*Works,* 20:26–27). Although Ruskin's purchases for the Sheffield museum of the Guild of Saint George would include some original artworks and copies for instructing the working classes, they were mixed together with mineral specimens, manuscripts, and other items. In John Rosenberg's view, Ruskin's entire contribution to the museum constituted "at once an expression of his principles and an evasion of his duties as Master" because it diverted him "from the management of the Guild's lands, which, after all, were its *raison d'être*" (197n). For an account of Ruskin's museological practices stressing his forward-looking emphasis on white walls, overhead lighting, generous spacing, and single-tier display, see Casteras.
12. The conventional belief about Whistler's motivation in bringing the libel suit against Ruskin has long been that Ruskin's published attack in *Fors Clavigera* had so jeopardized Whistler's ability to sell pictures that he was driven to seek redress at law. But Linda Merrill has assembled convincing evidence that this notion, popularized by Whistler's devoted biographers Joseph and Elizabeth Pennell, is not credible. Rather, Whistler's impecuniousness constituted the cause of his suit. The £1,000 Whistler hoped to gain in damages was meant to rescue him from a financial situation that had already become desperate: in the week before Whistler read Ruskin's review, his impatient creditors had thoroughly frightened him by sending a bailiff to his door demanding payment (see Merrill, 60–71, 279).
13. Whistler's *Nocturne* belonged to a series of Thames riverscapes he produced in the

early 1870s that frequently took as their focus the fireworks displays given at Cremorne Gardens, which had become by that time a notorious cruising ground for debauchees and prostitutes.

14. Whistler claimed that the following passage was libelous: "For Mr. Whistler's own sake, no less than for the protection of the purchaser, Sir Coutts Lindsay [the proprietor of the Grosvenor Gallery where the exhibition was held] ought not to have admitted works into the gallery in which the ill-educated conceit of the artist so nearly approached the aspect of wilful imposture. I have seen, and heard, much of Cockney impudence before now but never expected to hear a coxcomb ask two hundred guineas for flinging a pot of paint in the public's face" (*Works,* 29:160).
15. Ruskin had suffered a fierce attack of mental disease in February 1878, and although by September he wrote Charles Eliot Norton that "you need not be seriously fearful for me any more" (*Correspondence of John Ruskin,* 414), Ruskin's doctors continued watchful, ultimately advising him against participating in the Whistler trial. See also Merrill, 95–97.
16. Cf. Charles Kingsley's novel, *Alton Locke* (1850): "Truly, pictures are the books of the unlearned, and of the mis-learned too. Glorious Raffaelle! Shakespeare of the south! Mighty preacher, to whose blessed intuition it was given to know all human hearts, to embody in form and colour all spiritual truths, common alike to Protestant and Papist, to workman and to sage" (355).
17. In fact Whistler had been expelled from West Point, was the son of an American civil engineer, and had been born in the mill town of Lowell, Massachusetts. He apparently saw fit to lie about his origins while under oath on the witness stand: "I . . . was born at St. Petersburg" (Merrill, 141). Whistler's racism and anti-Semitism, by contrast, seem to have been entirely genuine.

III. The Brotherly Company of Art

1. For the period 1855–71 Morris enjoyed an income averaging £553 a year from stock in a Devonshire copper mining firm he had inherited from his father (see Harvey and Press, 23–25).
2. "That thing which I understand by real art," Morris declared in "The Art of the People" (1879), "is the expression by man of his pleasure in labour. I do not believe he can be happy in labour without expressing that happiness; and especially is this so when he is at work at anything in which he specially excels. A most kind gift is this of nature, since all men, nay, it seems all things too, must labour; so that not only does the dog take pleasure in hunting, and the horse in running, and the bird in flying, but so natural does the idea seem to us, that we imagine to ourselves that the earth and the very elements rejoice in doing their appointed work" (*Works,* 22:42).

   Morris was transferring an originally Christian notion of an acute delight in fulfilling one's allotted part in the plenitude of creation to a naturalistic account of being (see Sussman, 106–7). Morris's insistence on the legitimate claims of physical, bodily life would never falter. See, for instance, his "How We Live and How We Might Live" (1888): "To feel mere life a pleasure; to enjoy the moving one's limbs and exercising one's bodily powers; to play, as it were, with sun and wind and rain; to rejoice in satisfying the due bodily appetites of a human animal without fear of degradation or sense of wrong-doing: yes, and therewithal to be well-formed, straight-limbed, strongly knit, expressive of countenance—to be, in a word, beautiful—that also I claim" (*Works,* 23:17).

3. In 1883 Morris answered a correspondent who sought work on behalf of a promising young man that there was no employment at Morris and Company in craft work, where the men took their own sons as apprentices, or in "my own special work, designing for these crafts," because "somehow I have never been able to accept any help in it" (*Letters,* 2A:178).
4. "He was a keen judge and examiner of work, and fastidious, and as he did not mind taking trouble himself, he expected it from those who worked for him. His artistic influence was really due to the way he supervised work under his control, carried out by many different craftsmen under his eye, and not so much by his own actual handiwork" (Crane, 93).
5. To a certain degree Morris clearly was aware of the problem. He wrote in 1885 that it had been "almost impossible to do more than to insure the designer (mostly myself) some pleasure in his art by getting him to understand the qualities of materials and the happy chances of processes. Except with a small part of the more artistic side of the work, I could not do anything (or at least but little) to give this pleasure to the workmen, because I should have had to change their method of work so utterly that I should have disqualified them from earning their living elsewhere" (*Letters,* 2B:395).

   For all its apparent sincerity, however, some of Morris's admirers found this rationalization exasperating. In 1884, for example, the idealistic young bookbinder T. J. Cobden-Sanderson and his wife urged Morris to raise the pay of his workmen: "We told him we thought he ought to put his principles into practice in his own case, that his appeal would be much more powerful if he did so. He said he was in a corner and could not, that no one person could; that, to say the truth, he was a coward and feared to do so; that there was his wife, and the girls; and how could he put it upon them? . . . Dear old Morris, he would be happier if he could put his ideas into practice. But how shall the world be reformed if those who have ideas of the new State do not put their ideas into practice now, as far as they can? He said if he were to pay his workmen higher, they would all at once become capitalists. But this objection, I confess, seemed to be the objection of a man who had to look about for reasons" (Cobden-Sanderson, 1:174).
6. Morris's inextricable enmeshment in the contradictions of his own aesthetic capitalism has been extensively discussed by commentators. See, in particular, Hough, 96–101; Henderson, 368–69; Spear, 216–18; Freedman, 59–62; Harvey and Press, 154–56, 171–73.
7. In his 1884 lecture, "Textile Fabrics," Morris declared that any utopian ornamental art "may be in rather a Spartan way at first" (*Works,* 22:295). Wilfrid Scawen Blunt used the word *primitive* about Morris's style of life at Kelmscott Manor in Oxfordshire. Cobden-Sanderson described the rooms there as being "all spare of furniture, and having only what is necessary, strips of carpets, etc." (1:180); the designer W. R. Lethaby said that Morris "lived there in the summer in a delightful scrubbed table and whitewashed wall sort of way" (May Morris, 2:363). The daughter of the *Punch* artist Lindley Sambourne visited in the 1890s: "The house is lovely for its oldness but oh! *so so* artistic & grubby. The tea was laid out in a barbaric fashion

with a loaf on the table and a dirty jam pot that had been broken open through the paper at the top and the spoon looked too sticky to touch. We did not accept the tea but sat in a row in the plain *painfully* plain dining room & stared at Miss Morris and wondered why she dressed in such a sloppy way with no stays" (Nicholson, 154).

8. In his late essay "How I Became a Socialist" (1894) Morris identified "Whiggery" with complacent middle-class progressivism and moral-aesthetic obtuseness: "Before the uprising of *modern* Socialism almost all intelligent people either were, or professed themselves to be, quite contented with the civilization of this century. Again, almost all of these really were thus contented, and saw nothing to do but to perfect the said civilization by getting rid of a few ridiculous survivals of the barbarous ages. To be short, this was the *Whig* frame of mind, natural to the modern prosperous middle-class men, who, in fact, as far as mechanical progress is concerned, have nothing to ask for, if only Socialism would leave them alone to enjoy their plentiful style." Opposed to the regime of supremely blind content of "the said Whiggery," added Morris, there had arisen only two men: Carlyle and Ruskin (*Works,* 22:279).

   By 1899, however, Morris's younger contemporaries, Robert Steele and W. R. Lethaby, recognized in his opposition to Whiggery a new form of Tory Radicalism: "It was the taste for order and social harmony, and love of beauty, feelings essentially aristocratic and artistic, that drove him into revolt against the social anarchy which is the result of Whig *laissez-faire* under democratic conditions, when he compared it with the regulated economy which was the theory of medieval life." They concluded their analysis of Morris in the terms Wilde had already made familiar in *The Soul of Man under Socialism:* "We are inclined to hazard the paradox that, if Morris was a Socialist, he was so just because he was so intense an individualist" (589).

   For an argument that in the nineteenth century both Tory neomedievalists like Ruskin and Radical neo-medievalists like Morris were "romantic" mutants "of an essentially Whig stock," see Pocock, "Burke's Analysis," 211.

9. The idea of "divine discontent" was a favorite notion with Morris (see, for instance, *Works,* 22:424), who took it over from an 1874 essay by Charles Kingsley entitled "The Science of Health." In Kingsley, "divine discontent" is inward and Stoic—the wise man "will learn, like Epictetus" to be "discontented with no man and no thing save himself" ("Science of Health," 21)—whereas in Morris the discontent is directed outward toward the existing sociopolitical order. Pater would revive the older, more inward notion of discontent in *Marius the Epicurean* (1885), where the narrator says, "Surely the aim of a true philosophy must lie, not in futile efforts towards the complete accommodation of man to the circumstances in which he chances to find himself, but in the maintenance of a kind of candid discontent, in the face of the very highest achievement" (2:220). Wilde, in turn, would pursue Morris's romantic-activist notion of discontent: one of the characters in *A Woman of No Importance,* for instance, declares, "Discontent is the first step in the progress of a man or a nation."

10. Mackail regarded Morris's journeys to Iceland as possessing "an importance in Morris's life which can hardly be over-estimated" (1:240), and later commentators have concurred. Frederick Kirchhoff gives a particularly fine analysis of the meaning of Iceland to Morris during this period in his *William Morris* (86–89). Morris voiced his

hostility to the south, especially to Italy, in an 1878 letter written in Verona (see *Letters,* 1:486–87).

11. During his second trip to Iceland, Morris faced and overcame his paralyzing fear of crossing the "dreaded pass," the precipitous Bülandshöfði Pass (see *Works,* 8:122–23, 133).
12. Edward Thompson quotes a letter of March 1889 in which Morris declared, "I am now paying for the [Socialist] League (including paper) at the rate of £500 a year, and I cannot stand it" (520). In May 1896 Morris sent Sidney Cockerell with a blank check to Stuttgart to inspect a twelfth-century bestiary, which Cockerell bought for £700. Burne-Jones gave a characteristically winsome description of the scene as Cockerell returned with the book to Kelmscott Manor, "where Mr. Morris was—who wouldn't open it when he first saw it but handed it to [F. S.] Ellis who was there, and when Ellis had looked at it he said 'It's not a dear book, it's cheap.' Then Mr. Morris took it, and in ten minutes his heart was aglow" (Lago, 103).
13. See Morris's remark in an 1884 lecture: "In looking forward towards any utopia of the arts, I do not conceive to myself of there being a very great quantity of art of any kind, certainly not of ornament, apart from the purely intellectual arts; and even those must not swallow up too much of life" (*Works,* 22:294).
14. Perry Anderson has argued that Morris's demotion of intellectual labor in Nowhere "would have been unthinkable for Marx," who held that "'knowledge' was itself a fundamental and illimitable human 'desire'" (167).

IV. The Aristocracy of the Aesthetic

1. About this time, the American essayist Edwin Percy Whipple observed of "this hateful perversion of the true creed" of culture, "There is a class of educated readers in England and the United States" who having "generally 'gone through college' without having college go through them, are prone to pride themselves on their culture, and resent the most diffident criticisms regarding the perfection of their idol, Matthew Arnold, whom they look up to as the apostle of culture." Arnold's insistence on the importance of culture, Whipple concluded, "is in danger of being so perverted as to end practically 'in the culture of self-importance'" (294, 295).
2. Morris's sense of his own complicity in Aestheticist attitudes may be found in an 1888 essay, "The Revival of Handicraft," where he attempted to distance himself from them: "I must at the outset disclaim the mere aesthetic point of view which looks upon the ploughman and his bullocks and his plough, the reaper, his work, his wife, and his dinner, as so many elements which compose a pretty tapestry hanging, fit to adorn the study of a contemplative person of cultivation" (*Works,* 22:332). Just a few years earlier, Morris wrote a letter to Georgiana Burne-Jones that described the September wheat harvest at Kelmscott Manor in precisely the same terms he deprecated in this essay: "It has been a great pleasure to see man and maid so hard at work carrying [the wheat harvest] at last. Hobbs [the farmer who rented Kelmscott to Morris] began it on Wednesday morning, and by the next morning the thatchers were putting on the bright straw cap to the new rick: yesterday they were carrying the wheat in the field along our causeway and stacking it in our yard: pretty as one sat in the tapestry room to see the loads coming on between the stone walls" (*Letters,* 2A:62–63).

3. I am quoting from the 1873 version of the "Conclusion," which, due to the attacks upon it, Pater first omitted (1877) and then amended in later editions. Pater's response to the attacks led by such Tories as W. J. Courthope began, Gerald C. Monsman has noted (*Walter Pater's Art,* 152–53), in "Romanticism" (Nov. 1876), which specifically answers Courthope's "Wordsworth and Gray" (Jan. 1876), and continued through *Marius the Epicurean* and *Gaston de Latour.* Although Courthope published his essays anonymously in the *Quarterly Review,* his authorship of them was known to J. A. Symonds and thus probably to Pater.
4. Morley's complete phrase about these men, all of whom had attended Oxford—"the great current of *reactionary* force which the Oxford movement first released" (emphasis added)—demands to be understood in the context of Arnold's famous portrayal of the "sentiment of Oxford" in *Culture and Anarchy* (*Prose Works,* 5:87–256) and the preface to *Essays in Criticism,* first series. In these pieces, Arnold argues that the role of Oxford generally and of Newman and Hurrell Froude's Oxford Movement particularly was reactionary in a special sense—the "sentiment of Oxford" subversively resisting the present in the name of the past to benefit the future: "We have not won our political battles, we have not carried our main points, we have not stopped our adversaries' advance, we have not marched victoriously with the modern world; but we have told silently upon the mind of the country, we have prepared currents of feeling which sap our adversaries' position when it seems gained, we have kept up our own communications with the future" (*Prose Works,* 5:106).
5. For Symonds, see Dale's "Beyond Humanism." Emilia Pattison would later, as Lady Dilke, attribute the French Revolution itself to a smoldering resentment over the suppression in France of the earlier "revolution which we call the Renaissance" (*Art,* 220). For the idea of the Renaissance as a construction of nineteenth-century "interests and ideologies," see Fraser.
6. For Courthope's definition of Romanticism, see "The State of English Poetry," 36; for liberalism, see his "Modern Culture," 412–13.
7. See the recent books on Pater by Jonathan Freedman, Jonathan Loesberg, F. C. McGrath, Perry Meisel, Gerald C. Monsman, and Carolyn Williams. Notable exceptions to this prevailing critical emphasis can be found in the work of Peter Allan Dale and B. A. Inman.
8. For a fuller analysis of this transformation, see Linda Dowling, *Hellenism and Homosexuality in Victorian Oxford.* The standard account of Mill's influence on Oxford is Christopher Harvie's *Lights of Liberalism.* For the "Ultra Liberal" atmosphere at Oxford in which Pater came to intellectual maturity, see also Richter; Monsman, "Old Mortality"; Seiler, *Walter Pater: A Life Remembered,* 11–13; and Dellamora, 59–61.
9. "The better sort of journalists," declared Morley in his obituary essay on Mill, "educated themselves on his books, and even the baser sort acquired a habit of quoting from them" (670).
10. Quoted in Collini, *Public Moralists,* 178. Collini gives a finely nuanced account of the varying degrees of enthusiasm and adherence found among Mill's mid- and late-century followers.
11. Pater invoked the high humanist theme of *quidquid agunt homines,* for instance, in his essay on "Pico della Mirandola": "Nothing which has ever interested living men and women can wholly lose its vitality—no language they have spoken nor oracle

beside which they have hushed their voices, no dream which has once been entertained by actual human minds, nothing about which they have ever been passionate, or expended time and zeal" (*Renaissance,* 38). This theme became the implicit basis for recovering such vanished cultural forms as the paiderastic eros of ancient Greece.

12. Wages and salaries rose sharply in Britain during the third quarter of the nineteenth century. Even when this rise leveled off after the mid-1870s, the middle-class standard of living continued to improve dramatically due to the fall in prices for imported goods, domestic labor, and manufactured luxuries, with prices falling by about 40 percent between 1874 and 1896 (Harvey and Press, 77). While the situation of the poorest classes deteriorated and the nobility and landed gentry suffered from the effects of the great agricultural depression that began in the early 1870s, the middle classes continued to prosper from the boom in trade, commerce, manufacturing, and banking.
13. "Goethe's profound, imperturbable naturalism," Arnold declared in "Heinrich Heine" (1863), "is absolutely fatal to all routine thinking; he puts the standard, once for all, inside every man instead of outside him; when he is told, such a thing must be so, there is immense authority and custom in favour of its being so, it has been held to be so for a thousand years, he answers with Olympian politeness, 'But *is* it so? is it so to *me?*'" (*Prose Works,* 3:110).
14. Shaftesbury's *sensus communis*—the universally held capacity for moral and aesthetic judgment that is simultaneously an instinctive social sympathy—is the sustaining metaphysical premise behind what it has been customary to call Pater's moral aesthetic. Shaftesburian moral-sense theory, continuously translating the imperatives of duty into the affections of taste, declares itself openly whenever one of Pater's speakers meditates, for instance, on the "purely aesthetic beauty of the old morality," fascinating "to the imagination, to good taste in its most highly developed form" (*Marius,* 2:7), considers "those *manners* which are, in the deepest as in the simplest sense, *morals*" ("Wordsworth," 61), or says of Botticelli "his morality is all sympathy" (*Renaissance,* 43). Inman has determined that Pater borrowed Shaftesbury's *Characteristics* from the Brasenose College library in the autumn of 1869 (*Walter Pater's Reading,* 213). Wilde echoed Pater's thought when he said of Christ in *De Profundis,* "His morality is all sympathy, just what morality should be" (485).
15. Inman has attempted to explain Pater's metaphor of the focus in terms of Victorian experiments with limelight in "Intellectual Context," 22–24.
16. Pater's own review of Symonds's *Renaissance* (a review of volume 1 published in 1875) must be read as a complex act of simultaneous encouragement and caution made to a fellow liberal. For the emancipation inaugurated by the Renaissance is only valuable, Pater reminded Symonds, insofar as its assertion of liberty is the "liberty to see and feel those things the seeing and feeling of which generate not the 'barbarous ferocity of temper, the savage and coarse tastes' of the Renaissance Popes, but a sympathy with life everywhere even in its weakest and most frail manifestations" ("Review," 198; Pater was quoting from Symonds, who had appeared to revel in the savage aspect of the Italian Renaissance). "Sympathy, appreciation, a sense of latent claims in things which even good men pass rudely by," Pater continued, "on the whole are the characteristic traits of [Renaissance] artists" (198–99).

    Pater's stress on the powers of human sympathy awakened in the Renaissance represented, as Donald Hill pointed out in his edition, another theme taken over from Michelet. In volume 7 of his *Histoire de France,* for instance, Michelet declared, "*A world of humanity, of universal sympathy begins.* Man is finally the brother of the world. . . . There is the true meaning of the Renaissance: tenderness, kindness toward nature" (Pater, *Renaissance,* 462). At the same time, as Helen H. Young long ago argued, Pater's stress on sympathy derived at a fundamental level from the indigenous British political and philosophical traditions and in particular from the moral sense and benevolist schools originating with Shaftesbury that later came to be absorbed in some varieties of nineteenth-century utilitarianism and scientism. "One concept recurs in Pater's essays," Young declared, "which marked him the more clearly 'liberal' in the eyes of some of his contemporaries, in that it allied him to the positivists, to Darwin, Huxley, and Spencer. . . . This is the concept of *sympathy*" (47).

17. Botticelli was unappreciated in England until Pater—and following his lead, Ruskin—undertook his rehabilitation (see Kermode, 3–31, and Weinberg). Within a few years, however, Botticelli became a valuable part of an ambitious late Victorian's cultural capital, as Logan Pearsall Smith suggests when he says that the single sentence he remembered from a Harvard lecture given by Edmund Gosse in 1884 was "Botticelli, that name which is an open sesame to the most select, the most distinguished, the most exclusive circles of European culture" (122). Smith later discovered that Gosse's only real acquaintance with Botticelli at the time of his lecture derived from the satiric cartoons in *Punch.* By 1897 this "vulgarization" of Botticelli would be complete, the art writer and editor Gleeson White protesting that "when the world at large ridiculed both [i.e., Botticelli and Robert Browning], it was a proof of Culture to proclaim yourself of the minority. Now, when the 'Primavera' is in most drawing-rooms of the suburbs" and "when reproductions by all sorts of processes, from chromolithography to the meanest half-tone, are scattered everywhere, it is easier to smile at the craze, and convey an idea that an undue fondness for Botticelli denotes a lack of sympathy for real master-work" (82).
18. Kevin H. F. O'Brien showed that because "The English Renaissance" was too "theoretical" to please his audiences, Wilde used it "for only the first month of his tour and even during that short time emended it drastically. He made his second lecture, 'The Decorative Arts,' more practical and it became the lecture of the remaining nine months of the tour." Wilde saved the lecture entitled "The House Beautiful" for those occasions when he gave a second lecture in a city (395). O'Brien has determined that the two lectures that Robert Ross titled "Art and the Handicraftsman" and "House Decoration" when he published them in his 1908 edition of Wilde's works in fact represent, respectively, earlier and later versions of "The Decorative Arts."
19. "If England were swallowed up by the sea tomorrow, which of the two, a hundred years hence," as Arnold asked in *Culture and Anarchy,* "would most excite the love, interest, and admiration of mankind,—would most, therefore, show the evidences of having possessed greatness,—the England of the last twenty years, or the England of Elizabeth, of a time of splendid spiritual effort, but when our coal, and our industrial operations depending on coal, were very little developed?" (*Prose Works,* 5:97). Coleridge in *On the Constitution of Church and State* (1830) insisted that the "civilization" of a nation, much more than its fleets, armies, and revenue, "forms the ground of its defensive and offensive power" (10:43).
20. In "Art and the Handicraftsman," for example, Wilde declared that "the grandest art

of the world always came from a republic, Athens, Venice, and Florence—there were no kings there and so their art was as noble and simple as sincere" (*Complete Works,* 10:299), and in Louisville, Kentucky, he told a reporter, "I am a thorough republican. No other form of government is so favorable to the growth of art" (Ellmann, 196). Both sentiments reaffirm the familiar Whig claim that political liberty also liberates the arts.

21. Brushing aside all Pater's careful qualifications and reserve, Wilde portrayed the modern English Renaissance in precisely the political terms that Courthope had sought to expose as a scandal. Thus, where Pater had demoted and obscured Michelet's reference to "la Révolution" as "revolution," Wilde boldly insisted that "it is to the French Revolution"—that "great Revolution of which we are all the children" ("English Renaissance," in *Prose Works,* 10:245)—that we must look for the most primary factor and the first condition of the English Renaissance of art, namely, the "desire for perfection" (249). Where Pater had allowed his intense desire for "that more liberal way of life we have been seeking so long" to remain a momentous implication within his portrayal of the Renaissance, Wilde by contrast would burst out with a grandiose confidence to the Americans: "I want to make this artistic movement the basis for a new civilization" (*Omaha Weekly Herald,* 24 Mar. 1882, printed in Mikhail, *Interviews,* 1:58).
22. Something of Pater's acute, "tyrannous" sensitivity to visual beauty is expressed in the epiphany of the red hawthorn episode in "The Child in the House" (*Miscellaneous Studies,* 184–86). Wilde's intense responsiveness to beauty and ugliness, especially of persons, is described by Sherard, who believed it sincere but wildly excessive (see 55–56).
23. Collini remarked of this "at first sight somewhat heterogeneous" series of adjectives that it may be surprising to meet "a term like 'professional' in this list, since we may have come to think of it as an entirely positive quality." By placing the word *professional* in such a series, however, Arnold meant to draw "attention to the sense in which it represents a very questionable value." What links these terms, Collini observed, was Arnold's idea that knowledge should not be "imprisoned in a form of expression that is specialized, technical, idiosyncratic, or private, but should rather be accessible, shareable, public" (*Arnold,* 86–87). Collini's remark serves, in the face of recent commentary asserting the "professional" character of the aesthete (see, for instance, Freedman, xix, xxvi, 52–58) as a salutary reminder of the deeply equivocal meaning of *professional* among the Victorians, for whom its disparaging connotations of a narrow, vendible expertise were reinforced by the implicit contrast to the ideal of the equally skillful but always unremunerated amateur in the social traditions of the English gentry and aristocracy (see the *Oxford English Dictionary*'s definition of *professional,* 2:4).
24. Insisting that "questions of titles are matters of heraldry—no more," Wilde attempted in vain to rid Lord Alfred Douglas of "his absurd and ridiculous assumption of social superiority" (*Letters,* 624). Wilde considered Douglas, the third son of a Scotch marquess, to be "a young man of my own social rank and position" (433) and in no way the superior of any gentleman, much less a poet and man of genius. The late-twentieth-century conviction that Wilde must have gone through life, in the words of one recent biographical study, "smarting under the idea that he was not an aristocrat" (Knox, 106), would have, one suspects, simply astounded him.
25. Throughout *The Critic as Artist,* as when Gilbert declares that "the mission of the

aesthetic movement is to lure people to contemplate, not to lead them to create" (*The Artist as Critic,* 396), Wilde translates Plato's remarks on philosophy to the autonomous realm of art as such. For a similar displacement involving Aristotle, see *Oscar Wilde's Oxford Notebooks,* 145.

26. These works were first entered as evidence during the libel trial Wilde brought against the marquess of Queensberry as proof that Queensberry had indeed been justified in calling Wilde a sodomite. Subsequently, the two works were introduced in the two criminal trials as evidence of Wilde's "gross indecency." During the libel trial Wilde defended these writings in Millian terms. The defense counsel for Queensberry asked if such paradoxical epigrams as "Religions die when they are proved to be true" were good for young men to read. "Anything is good," Wilde replied, "that stimulates thought in whatever age" (Hyde, 123).
27. See Ellmann, 450–51, 462, 465. Some recent commentators (see, for instance, Gagnier, 205–7, and Dellamora, 194–99, 210–12), accepting Lord Alfred Douglas's conspiracy theory of Wilde's prosecution at the hands of the Liberals, have been inclined to portray his prosecution as a show trial motivated by Victorian homophobia.

Works Cited

Abrams, M. H. "Kant and the Theology of Art." *Notre Dame English Journal* 13 (1981): 75–106.

Adams, Francis. "Democracy: A Dialogue." In his *Essays in Modernity,* 43–82. London: John Lane, 1899.

Anderson, Perry. *Arguments within English Marxism.* London: Verso, 1980.

apRoberts, Ruth. "Arnold and the Cambridge Platonists." *Clio* 17 (1988): 139–50.

Arbuckle, James. *A Collection of Letters and Essays on Several Subjects.* 2 vols. London, 1729; rpt. New York: Garland, 1970.

Armstrong, John. "Taste: An Epistle to a Young Critic" (1753). In *Miscellanies,* ed. Ralph Cohen. Augustan Reprint Society no. 30. Los Angeles: William Andrews Clark Memorial Library, 1951.

Arnold, Matthew. "Bishop Butler and the Zeit-Geist." In *Prose Works,* 8:11–62.

———. *The Complete Prose Works of Matthew Arnold,* ed. R. H. Super. 11 vols. Ann Arbor: Univ. of Michigan Press, 1960–77.

———. *Culture and Anarchy.* In *Prose Works,* 5:87–256.

———. "Heinrich Heine." *Prose Works,* 3:107–32.

———. *Letters of Matthew Arnold, 1848–1888,* ed. George W. E. Russell. 2 vols. London: Macmillan, 1895.

———. "On the Modern Element in Literature." *Macmillan's Magazine* 19 (Feb. 1869): 304–14.

Barrell, John. "'The Dangerous Goddess': Masculinity, Prestige, and the Aesthetic in Early Eighteenth-Century Britain." *Cultural Critique* 12 (1989): 101–31.

———. *The Political Theory of Painting from Reynolds to Hazlitt: "The Body of the Public."* New Haven: Yale Univ. Press, 1986.

Beatty, Michael. "A Pot of Paint in the Public's Face: Ruskin's Censure of Whistler Reconsidered." *English Studies in Africa* 30 (1987): 27–41.

Bellamy, Edward. *Looking Backward.* Ed. John L. Thomas. Cambridge: Harvard Univ. Press, 1967.

Blunt, Wilfrid Scawen. *My Diaries: Being a Personal Narrative of Events 1888–1914.* 2 vols. London: Martin Secker, 1921.

Bourdieu, Pierre. *Distinction: A Social Critique of the Judgment of Taste,* trans. Richard Nice. Cambridge: Harvard Univ. Press, 1984.

Brake, Laurel, and Ian Small, eds. *Pater in 1990s.* Greensboro, N.C.: ELT Press, 1991.

Brantlinger, Patrick. "'News from Nowhere': Morris' Socialist Anti-Novel." *Victorian Studies* 19 (1975): 35–50.

Bürger, Peter. *Theory of the Avant-Garde.* Trans. Michael Shaw. Minneapolis: Univ. of Minnesota Press, 1984.

Burke, Edmund. *A Philosophical Enquiry into the Origin of Our Ideas of the Sublime and the Beautiful.* Ed. J. T. Boulton. Notre Dame, Ind.: Univ. of Notre Dame Press, 1968.

Burne-Jones, Georgiana. *Memorials of Edward Burne-Jones.* 2 vols. London: Macmillan, 1906.

Burrow, J. W. *Whigs and Liberals: Continuity and Change in English Political Thought.* Oxford: Clarendon, 1988.

Carlyle, Thomas. "Characteristics." In *The Works of Thomas Carlyle,* 23:00–00. London: Chapman and Hall, 1899; rpt. New York: AMS Press, 1969.

———. *The Collected Letters of Jane Welsh and Thomas Carlyle,* ed. Charles F. Harrold et al. Vol. 1. Durham, N.C.: Duke Univ. Press, 1956.

———. "Shooting Niagara—And after?" In *Scottish and Other Critical Miscellanies,* ed. James Russell Lowell, 299–339. London: J. W. Dent, 1915.

Carr, C. T. "The German Influence in the English Vocabulary." *Society for Pure English Tract* no. 42. Oxford: Clarendon, 1934.

Carritt, E. F. "The Sources and Effects in England of Kant's Philosophy of Beauty." *Monist* 35 (1925): 315–28.

Carter, Allan Loraine. *Parallel Themes and Their Treatment in Schiller and Shaftesbury.* Philadelphia: n.p., 1919.

Cassirer, Ernst. "Schiller und Shaftesbury." *Publications of the English Goethe Society* n.s. 11 (1935): 37–59.

Casteras, Susan P. "'The Germ of a Museum, Arranged First for "Workers in Iron"': Ruskin's Museological Theories and the Curating of the Saint George's Museum." In *John Ruskin and the Victorian Eye,* 184–209. New York: Harry N. Abrams, 1993.

Cate, George Allen, ed. *The Correspondence of Thomas Carlyle and John Ruskin.* Stanford, Calif.: Stanford Univ. Press, 1982.

Cavell, Stanley. *The Senses of Walden.* San Francisco: North Point, 1981.

Caygill, Howard. *The Art of Judgment.* Oxford: Basil Blackwell, 1989.

Chytry, Josef. *The Aesthetic State: A Quest in Modern German Thought.* Berkeley: Univ. of California Press, 1989.

Cobden-Sanderson, Thomas James. *The Journals of T. J. Cobden-Sanderson: 1879–1922.* 2 vols. New York: Macmillan, 1926.

Coleman, Stephen. "A Rejoinder to Barbara Gribble." *Journal of the William Morris Society* 7 (1986): 36–39.

Coleridge, Samuel Taylor. *On the Constitution of Church and State.* Ed. John Colmer. In *The Collected Works of Samuel Taylor Coleridge,* ed. Kathleen Coburn, 10:5–161. Princeton: Princeton Univ. Press, 1976.

Collingwood, R. G. "Plato's Philosophy of Art." *Mind* 34 (1925): 154–72.

Collini, Stefan. *Arnold.* Oxford: Oxford Univ. Press, 1988.

———. Introduction to *The Collected Works of John Stuart Mill,* ed. John M. Robson, 21:vii–lvi. Toronto: Univ. of Toronto Press, 1984.

———. *Public Moralists: Political Thought and Intellectual Life in Britain 1850–1930*. Oxford: Clarendon, 1993.

Colvin, Sidney. "Literature and the Manual Arts." *Fortnightly Review,* o.s. 33, n.s. 27 (Apr. 1880): 580–97.

Compton-Rickett, Arthur. *William Morris: A Study in Personality.* London, 1913; rpt. Port Washington, N.Y.: Kennikat, 1972.

Cornish, F. W. "Greek Beauty and Modern Art" *Fortnightly Review,* o.s. 20, n.s. 14 (Sept. 1873): 326–36.

Court, Franklin E. *Pater and His Early Critics*. Victoria, B.C.: English Literary Studies, 1980.

Courthope, W. J. "Modern Culture." *Quarterly Review* 137 (Oct. 1874): 389–415.

———. "The Renaissance in Italy and England." *Quarterly Review* 145 (Jan. 1877): 1–34.

———. "The Progress of Taste." *Quarterly Review* 149 (Jan. 1880): 47–83.

———. "The State of English Poetry." *Quarterly Review* 135 (July 1873): 1–40.

———. "Wordsworth and Gray." *Quarterly Review* 141 (Jan. 1876): 104–36.

Crane, Walter. "William Morris." *Scribner's* 22 (July 1897): 88–99.

Culler, A. Dwight. *The Victorian Mirror of History.* New Haven: Yale Univ. Press, 1985.

Dale, Peter Allan. "Beyond Humanism: J. A. Symonds and the Replotting of the Renaissance." *Clio* 17 (1988): 109–37.

———. "'Distractions of Spirit': Walter Pater and Modernity." *Papers in Literature and Language* 28 (1992): 319–49.

D'Amico, Masolino. "Oscar Wilde between 'Socialism' and Aestheticism." *English Miscellany* 18 (1967): 111–39.

Dawson, Carl. *Victorian Noon: English Literature in 1850*. Baltimore: Johns Hopkins Univ. Press, 1979.

DeLaura, David J. "The Context of Browning's Painter Poems: Aesthetics, Polemics, Historics." *Publications of the Modern Language Association* 95 (1980): 367–88.

Dellamora, Richard. *Masculine Desire: The Sexual Politics of Victorian Aestheticism*. Chapel Hill: Univ. of North Carolina Press, 1990.

Dilke, Emilia F. S. *Art in the Modern State*. London: Chapman and Hall, 1888.

Dollimore, Jonathan. "Different Desires: Subjectivity and Transgression in Wilde and Gide." *Genders* 2 (1988): 24–41.

Dowling, Linda. *Hellenism and Homosexuality in Victorian Oxford*. Ithaca: Cornell Univ. Press, 1994.

Dowling, William C. *Jameson, Althusser, Marx: An Introduction to "The Political Unconscious"*. Ithaca: Cornell Univ. Press, 1984.

Dunham, Barrows. *A Study in Kant's Aesthetics: The Universal Validity of Aesthetic Judgment*. Lancaster, Pa.: privately printed, 1934.

Dunn, John. "Consent in the Political Theory of John Locke." *Historical Journal* 10 (1967): 153–82.

Eagleton, Terry. *The Ideology of the Aesthetic.* New York: Basil Blackwell, 1990.

Eastlake, Elizabeth Rigby. "*Modern Painters.*" *Quarterly Review* 98 (Mar. 1856): 384–433.

Ellmann, Richard. *Oscar Wilde.* New York: Knopf, 1988.

Faulkner, Peter, ed. *William Morris: The Critical Heritage.* London: Routledge and Kegan Paul, 1973.

Fennell, Francis L. "The Verdict in Whistler v. Ruskin." *Victorian Newsletter* 40 (Fall 1971): 17–21.

Ferguson, Adam. *An Essay on the History of Civil Society.* Ed. Duncan Forbes. Edinburgh: Edinburgh Univ. Press, 1966.

Ferry, Luc. *Homo aestheticus: L'invention du goût à l'âge démocratique.* Paris: Grasset, 1990.

Filmer, Sir Robert. *Patriarcha and Other Political Works.* Ed. Peter Laslett. Oxford: Basil Blackwell, 1949.

Floud, Peter. "The Inconsistencies of William Morris." *Listener* 52 (1954): 615–17.

Fraser, Hilary. *The Victorians and Renaissance Italy.* Oxford: Basil Blackwell, 1992.

Freedman, Jonathan. *Professions of Taste: Henry James, British Aestheticism, and Commodity Culture.* Stanford, Calif.: Stanford Univ. Press, 1990.

Gagnier, Regenia. *Idylls of the Marketplace: Oscar Wilde and the Victorian Public.* Stanford, Calif.: Stanford Univ. Press, 1986.

Gallagher, Catherine. *The Industrial Reformation of English Fiction: Social Discourse and Narrative Form, 1832–1867.* Chicago: Univ. of Chicago Press, 1985.

Gilbert, Katharine. "Ruskin's Relation to Aristotle." *Philosophical Review* 49 (1940): 52–62.

Girard, René. *Violence and the Sacred.* Trans. Patrick Gregory. Baltimore: Johns Hopkins Univ. Press, 1977.

Gray, Thomas. *The Correspondence of Thomas Gray.* Ed. Paget Toynbee and Leonard Whibley. 3 vols. Oxford: Clarendon, 1935.

Gribble, Barbara. "William Morris's *News from Nowhere:* A Vision Impaired." *Journal of the William Morris Society* 6 (1985): 16–22.

Grigson, Geoffrey. "Pope of Art." *New Statesman* 67 (1964): 222–23.

Guyer, Paul. *Kant and the Claims of Taste.* Cambridge: Harvard Univ. Press, 1979.

Harris, Wendell V. "An Anatomy of Aestheticism." In *Victorian Literature and Society: Essays Presented to Richard D. Altick,* ed. James R. Kincaid and Albert J. Kuhn, 331–47. Columbus: Ohio State Univ. Press, 1984.

Harrison, Frederic. *John Ruskin.* New York: Macmillan, 1902.

———. "The Reaction and Its Lessons." *Fortnightly Review* o.s. 64, n.s. 58 (Oct. 1895): 485–96.

———. "The Subjective Synthesis." *Fortnightly Review* o.s. 14, n.s. 8 (Aug. 1870): 184–97.

Harvey, Charles, and Jon Press. *William Morris: Design and Enterprise in Victorian Britain.* Manchester: Manchester Univ. Press, 1991.

Harvie, Christopher. *The Lights of Liberalism: University Liberalism and the Challenge of Democracy, 1860–1886.* London: Lane, 1976.

Helsinger, Elizabeth K. *Ruskin and the Art of the Beholder.* Cambridge: Harvard Univ. Press, 1982.

Henderson, Philip. *William Morris: His Life, Work, and Friends.* London: Thames and Hudson, 1967.

Hewlett, Maurice. "A Materialist's Paradise" (1891). In *William Morris: The Critical Heritage,* ed. Peter Faulkner, 343–53. London: Routledge and Kegan Paul, 1973.

Hilton, Tim. *John Ruskin: The Early Years, 1819–1859.* New Haven: Yale Univ. Press, 1985.

Himmelfarb, Gertrude. "Liberty: 'One Very Simple Principle.'" *American Scholar* 62 (1993): 531–50.

Hough, Graham. *The Last Romantics.* London, 1947; rpt. New York: Barnes and Noble, 1961.

Hutcheson, Francis. *Inquiry into the Original of Our Ideas of Beauty and Virtue.* 2d ed. London: printed for J. Darby et al., 1726.

Hyde, H. Montgomery. *The Trials of Oscar Wilde.* London and Edinburgh: William Hodge, 1948.

Inman, B. A. "The Intellectual Context of Walter Pater's 'Conclusion.'" In *Walter Pater: An Imaginative Sense of Fact,* ed. Philip Dodd, pp. 12–30. London: Frank Cass, 1981.

———. *Walter Pater's Reading: A Bibliography of His Library Borrowings and Literary References, 1858–1873.* New York: Garland, 1981.

Ironside, Robin. "The Art Criticism of Ruskin." *Horizon* 8 (1943): 8–20.

Jameson, Fredric. *Marxism and Form: Twentieth-Century Dialectical Theories of Literature.* Princeton: Princeton Univ. Press, 1971.

Jowett, Benjamin. *The Life and Letters of Benjamin Jowett, M.A.* Ed. Evelyn Abbott and Lewis Campbell. 2 vols. London: John Murray, 1897.

Kant, Immanuel. *The Critique of Judgment.* Trans. James Creed Meredith. Oxford: Clarendon, 1952.

Kermode, Frank. *Forms of Attention.* Chicago: Univ. of Chicago Press, 1987.

Kingsley, Charles. *Alton Locke, Tailor and Poet: An Autobiography.* Ed. Elizabeth A. Cripps. New York: Oxford Univ. Press, 1983.

———. "The Science of Health." In his *Health and Education,* 1–25. London: W. Isbister, 1874.

Kirchhoff, Frederick. *William Morris.* Boston: Twayne, 1979.

———. "William Morris's Anti-Books: The Kelmscott Press and the Late Prose Romances." In *Forms of the Fantastic,* ed. Jan Hokenson and Howard Pearce, 93–100. New York: Greenwood, 1986.

Klein, Lawrence E. *Shaftesbury and the Culture of Politeness: Moral Discourse and Cultural Politics in Early Eighteenth-Century England.* Cambridge: Cambridge Univ. Press, 1994.

Knox, Melissa. *Oscar Wilde: A Long and Lovely Suicide.* New Haven: Yale Univ. Press, 1994.

Kristeller, Paul Oskar. "The Modern System of the Arts." In *Renaissance Thought II: Papers on Humanism and the Arts,* 163–227. New York: Harper and Row, 1965.

Lago, Mary, ed. *Burne-Jones Talking: His Conversations 1895–1898 Preserved by His Studio Assistant Thomas Rooke*. London: John Murray, 1982.

Landow, George. *The Aesthetic and Critical Theories of John Ruskin*. Princeton: Princeton Univ. Press, 1971.

———. "There Began to Be a Great Talking about the Fine Arts." In *The Mind and Art of Victorian England*, ed. Josef L. Altholz, 124–45. Minneapolis: Univ. of Minnesota Press, 1976.

Laslett, Peter. Introduction to John Locke, *Two Treatises of Government*, 3–122. Cambridge: Cambridge Univ. Press, 1980.

Levine, George. "Reclaiming the Aesthetic." In *Aesthetics and Ideology*, ed. George Levine, 1–28. New Brunswick, N.J.: Rutgers Univ. Press, 1994.

Locke, John. *An Essay Concerning Human Understanding*. Ed. Peter Nidditch. Oxford: Clarendon, 1975.

———. *Two Treatises of Government*. Ed. Peter Laslett. Cambridge: Cambridge Univ. Press, 1980.

Loesberg, Jonathan. *Aestheticism and Deconstruction: Pater, Derrida, and De Man*. Princeton: Princeton Univ. Press, 1991.

Lovejoy, A. O. "The Parallel of Deism and Classicism." *Modern Philology* 39 (1932): 281–99.

MacIntyre, Alasdair. *After Virtue*. 2d ed. Notre Dame, Ind.: Univ. of Notre Dame Press, 1984.

Mackail, J. W. *The Life of William Morris*. 2 vols. London: Longmans, Green, 1899.

McGrath, F. C. *The Sensible Spirit: Walter Pater and the Modernist Paradigm*. Tampa: Univ. of South Florida Press, 1986.

McMaster, Roland. "Tensions in Paradise: Anarchism, Civilization, and Pleasure in Morris's *News from Nowhere*." *English in Canada* 17 (1991): 73–87.

Mandeville, Bernard. *The Fable of the Bees, or Private Vices, Publick Benefits*. Ed. F. B. Kaye. 2 vols. Oxford: Clarendon, 1924.

Markley, Robert. "Sentimentality as Performance: Shaftesbury, Sterne, and the Theatrics of Virtue." In *The New Eighteenth Century: Theory, Politics, English Literature*, ed. Laura Brown and Felicity Nussbaum, 210–30. New York: Methuen, 1987.

———. "Style as Philosophical Structure: The Contexts of Shaftesbury's *Characteristics*." In *The Philosopher as Writer: The Eighteenth Century*, ed. Robert Ginsberg, 140–54. Cranbury, N.J.: Association of Univ. Presses for Susquehanna Univ. Press, 1987.

Marx, Karl. *Grundrisse: Foundations of the Critique of Political Economy*. Trans. Martin Nicolaus. New York: Vintage Books, 1973.

Meier, Paul. *William Morris: The Marxist Dreamer*. Trans. Frank Gubb. 2 vols. Atlantic Highland, N.J.: Harvester, 1978.

Melmoth, William. *Letters on Several Subjects of the Late Sir Thomas Fitzosborne, Published from the Copies Found among His Papers*. 2 vols. London, 1749; rpt. New York: Garland, 1971.

Meisel, Perry. *The Absent Father: Virginia Woolf and Walter Pater*. New Haven: Yale Univ. Press, 1980.

Merrill, Linda. *A Pot of Paint: Aesthetics on Trial in Whistler v. Ruskin.* Washington, D.C.: Smithsonian Institution Press, 1992.

Mikhail, E. H. *Oscar Wilde: Interviews and Recollections.* 2 vols. New York: Barnes and Noble, 1979.

Mill, John Stuart. *On Liberty.* In *The Collected Works of John Stuart Mill,* ed. John M. Robson, 18:213–310. Toronto: Univ. of Toronto Press, 1965–91.

Molesworth, Robert. *An Account of Denmark.* London: Printed for T. Goodwin, 1694.

Monsman, Gerald C. "Old Mortality at Oxford." *Studies in Philology* 67 (1970): 359–89.

———. *Walter Pater's Art of Autobiography.* New Haven: Yale Univ. Press, 1980.

Morley, John. "The Death of Mr. Mill" *Fortnightly Review* 13 (June 1873): 669–76.

———. "Mr. Pater's Essays." *Fortnightly Review* 13 (Apr. 1873): 468–77.

Morris, May. *William Morris: Artist, Writer, Socialist.* 2 vols. New York: Russell and Russell, 1966.

Morris, William. *The Collected Letters of William Morris,* ed. Norman Kelvin. 3 vols. Princeton: Princeton Univ., 1984–.

———. *The Collected Works of William Morris,* ed. May Morris. 24 vols. London: Longmans, 1910–15.

———. Preface to *The Nature of Gothic: A Chapter of* The Stones of Venice *by John Ruskin,* i–v. London: George Allen, 1892.

———. *The Unpublished Lectures of William Morris.* Ed. Eugene D. LeMire. Detroit: Wayne State Univ. Press, 1969.

Needham, Paul. "William Morris: Book Collector." In *William Morris and the Art of the Book,* ed. Paul Needham, Joseph Dunlap, and John Dreyfus, 21–47. New York: Pierpont Morgan Library, 1976.

Nicholson, Shirley. *A Victorian Household.* London: Barrie and Jenkins, 1988.

Nietzsche, Friedrich. *The Will to Power.* Trans. Walter Kaufmann and R. J. Hollingdale. New York: Vintage, 1968.

Norton, Charles Eliot. "Harvard." In *Four American Universities,* 3–43. New York: Harper, 1895.

———. *Notes of Travel and Study in Italy.* Boston, Ticknor and Fields, 1860; rpt. New York: Johnson, 1971.

Oakeshott, Michael. *Morality and Politics in Modern Europe: The Harvard Lectures.* Ed. Shirley Robin Letwin. New Haven: Yale Univ. Press, 1993.

O'Brien, Kevin H. F. "'The House Beautiful': A Reconstruction of Oscar Wilde's American Lecture." *Victorian Studies* 17 (1974): 395–418.

Oliphant, Margaret. Unsigned review of Walter Pater's *Renaissance. Blackwood's Magazine* 114 (Nov. 1873): 604–9.

Olivier, Sydney. "William Morris (Born March 24th, 1834)." *Spectator* 152 (1934): 440–41.

Original Letters of John Locke, Algernon Sidney, and Lord Shaftesbury. Ed. Thomas Forster. 2d ed. London: privately printed, 1847.

Orr, Linda. "French Romantic Histories of the Revolution: Michelet, Blanc, Tocqueville—A Narrative." In *The French Revolution, 1789–1989: Two Hundred Years of Rethinking,* ed. Sandy Petrey, 123–42. Lubbock: Texas Tech Univ. Press, 1989.

Palgrave, F. T. "The Decline of Art." *Nineteenth Century* 23 (Jan. 1888): 71–92.

Pascal, Roy. "'Bildung' and the Division of Labour." In *German Studies Presented to W. H. Bruford,* 14–28. London: Harrap, 1962.

Passmore, J. A. "The Dreariness of Aesthetics" *Mind* 60 (1951): 318–35.

Pater, Walter. "Coleridge's Writings." *Westminster Review* 29 (Jan. 1866): 106–32.

———. *Gaston de Latour: A Unfinished Romance.* 1888; London: Macmillan, 1910.

———. *Marius the Epicurean: His Sensations and Ideas.* 2 vols. London: Macmillan, 1910.

———. *Miscellaneous Studies.* London: Macmillan, 1920.

———. *Plato and Platonism.* London: Macmillan, 1910.

———. "Poems by William Morris." *Westminster Review* n.s. 34 (Oct. 1868): 300–312.

———. *The Renaissance: Studies in Art and Poetry: The 1893 Text.* Ed. Donald L. Hill. Berkeley: Univ. of California Press, 1980. Originally published as *Studies in the History of the Renaissance.* London: 1873.

———. Review of J. A. Symonds's *Renaissance in Italy: The Age of the Despots. Academy* 8 (July 1875): 105–6, in Pater, *The Renaissance,* 196–202.

———. "Romanticism." *Macmillan's Magazine* 35 (Nov. 1876): 164–70.

———. "Sebastian van Storck." In *Imaginary Portraits,* 81–115. London: Macmillan, 1910.

———. "Winckelmann." *Westminster Review* 87 (Jan. 1867): 36–50.

———. "Wordsworth" (1874). In his *Appreciations,* 39–64. London: Macmillan, 1910.

Pattison, Emilia F. S. Unsigned review of Walter Pater's *Renaissance. Westminster Review* n.s. 43 (Apr. 1873): 639–41.

Paulson, Ronald. *Breaking and Remaking: Aesthetic Practice in England, 1700–1820.* New Brunswick, N.J.: Rutgers Univ. Press, 1989.

Peterson, William S., ed. *The Ideal Book: Essays and Lectures on the Arts of the Book by William Morris.* Berkeley: Univ. of California Press, 1982.

Pocock, J. G. A. "Burke's Analysis of the French Revolution." In his *Virtue, Commerce, and History: Essays on Political Thought, Chiefly in the Eighteenth Century,* 193–212. Cambridge: Cambridge Univ. Press, 1985.

———. *The Machiavellian Moment: Florentine Political Thought and the Atlantic Republican Tradition.* Princeton: Princeton Univ. Press, 1975.

Poggioli, Renato. "*Qualis Artifex Pereo!* or Barbarism and Decadence." *Harvard Library Bulletin* 13 (1959): 135–59.

Pritchett, V. S. "The Most Solitary Victorian." *New Statesman* n.s. 52 (1956): 489–90.

Quiller-Couch, Arthur. "A Literary Causerie: Mr. William Morris" (1896). In *William Morris: The Critical Heritage,* ed. Peter Faulkner, 395–98. London: Routledge and Kegan Paul, 1973.

Review of Walter Pater's *Renaissance. Saturday Review* 36 (July 1873): 123–24.

Review of William Morris's *The Roots of the Mountains. Spectator* (Feb. 1890), in *William*

Morris: The Critical Heritage, ed. Peter Faulkner, 335–38. London: Routledge and Kegan Paul, 1973.

Richards, Thomas. *The Commodity Culture of Victorian England: Advertising and Spectacle, 1851–1914*. Stanford, Calif.: Stanford Univ. Press, 1990.

Richter, Melvin. *The Politics of Conscience: T. H. Green and His Age*. London: Weidenfeld and Nicolson, 1964.

Rorty, Richard. "Foucault/Dewey/Nietzsche." *Raritan* 9 (1990): 1–8.

Rosenberg, John D. *The Darkening Glass: A Portrait of Ruskin's Genius*. New York: Columbia Univ. Press, 1961.

Ruskin, John. *The Correspondence of John Ruskin and Charles Eliot Norton*. Ed. John Bradley and Ian Ousby. Cambridge: Cambridge Univ. Press, 1987.

———. *The Stones of Venice*. In *Works,* vols. 9–11.

———. *The Works of John Ruskin,* ed. E. T. Cook and Alexander Wedderburn. 39 vols. London: George Allen, 1903–12.

Sawyer, Paul L. *Ruskin's Poetic Argument: The Design of the Major Works*. Ithaca: Cornell Univ. Press, 1985.

Schiller, Friedrich. *On the Aesthetic Education of Man, in a Series of Letters*. Ed. Elizabeth M. Wilkinson and L. A. Willoughby. Oxford: Clarendon, 1982.

Scott, P. G. "An Early Use of 'Aesthetic.'" *Notes and Queries* n.s. 14 (1967): 380.

Seiler, R. M., ed. *Walter Pater: A Life Remembered*. Calgary, Alberta: Univ. of Calgary Press, 1987.

———. *Walter Pater: The Critical Heritage*. London and Boston: Routledge and Kegan Paul, 1980.

Shaftesbury, Anthony Ashley Cooper, third earl of. *Characteristics of Men, Manners, Opinions, Times, Etc.* Ed. John M. Robertson. 2 vols. London: Grant Richards, 1900.

———. *The Life, Unpublished Letters, and Philosophical Regimen of Anthony, Earl of Shaftesbury.* Ed. Benjamin Rand. London: Swan Sonnenschein; New York: Macmillan, 1900.

———. *Second Characters or the Language of Forms*. Ed. Benjamin Rand. Cambridge: Cambridge Univ. Press, 1914.

Sharp, Frank C. "Crossing the Generation Gap: The Relationship of William Holman Hunt with Edward Burne-Jones and William Morris." *Journal of Pre-Raphaelite Studies* n.s. 3 (1994): 25–33.

Sherard, Robert H. *Oscar Wilde: The Story of an Unhappy Friendship*. London, 1902; rpt. New York: Haskell, 1970.

Sherburne, James Clark. *John Ruskin or the Ambiguities of Abundance*. Cambridge: Harvard Univ. Press, 1972.

Sidgwick, Henry. *Outlines of the History of Ethics* (1886). 5th ed. London: Macmillan, 1902.

Silver, Carole G. "Socialism Internalized: The Last Romances of William Morris." In *Socialism and the Literary Artistry of William Morris,* ed. Florence Boos and Carole G. Silver, 117–26. Columbia: Univ. of Missouri Press, 1990.

Skinner, Quentin. "Meaning and Understanding in the History of Ideas." *History and Theory* 8 (1969): 3–53.

Smith, Goldwin. "The Experience of the American Commonwealth." In *Essays on Reform,* pp. 217–37. London: Macmillan, 1867.

Smith, Logan Pearsall. *Unforgotten Years.* Boston: Little, Brown, 1939.

Sparling, H. H. *The Kelmscott Press and William Morris, Master-Craftsman.* London: Macmillan, 1924.

Spear, Jeffrey L. *Dreams of an English Eden: Ruskin and His Tradition in Social Criticism.* New York: Columbia Univ. Press, 1984.

Stansky, Peter. *Redesigning the World: William Morris, the 1880s, and the Arts and Crafts.* Princeton: Princeton Univ. Press, 1985.

Steele, Robert, and W. R. Lethaby. "William Morris, Poet and Artist." *Quarterly Review* 190 (Oct. 1899): 487–512.

Stein, Richard. *The Ritual of Interpretation: The Fine Arts as Literature in Ruskin, Rossetti, and Pater.* Cambridge: Harvard Univ. Press, 1975.

Stephen, Leslie. "Shaftesbury's 'Characteristics.'" *Fraser's Magazine* o.s. 87, n.s. 7 (Jan. 1873): 76–93.

Stephens, F. G. Unsigned review of Walter Pater's *Renaissance. Athenaeum* (28 June 1873), in *Walter Pater: The Critical Heritage,* ed. R. M. Seiler, 78–81. London and Boston: Routledge and Kegan Paul, 1980.

Stolnitz, Jerome. "On the Origins of 'Aesthetic Disinterestedness.'" *Journal of Aesthetics and Art Criticism* 20 (1961): 131–43.

Sussman, Herbert. *Victorians and the Machine: The Literary Response to Technology.* Cambridge: Harvard Univ. Press, 1968.

Symonds, J. A. "*Studies in the History of the Renaissance* by Walter H. Pater." *Academy* 4 (Mar. 1873): 103–5.

Talbot, Norman. "'Whilom, as Tells the Tale': The Language of the Prose Romances." *Journal of the William Morris Society* 8 (1989): 16–26.

Tanner, Robin. "What William Morris Means to Me." *Journal of the William Morris Society* 7 (1987): 3–17.

Taylor, Charles. *Hegel.* Cambridge: Cambridge Univ. Press, 1975.

———. *Sources of the Self: The Making of the Modern Identity.* Cambridge: Harvard Univ. Press, 1989.

Thompson, E. P. *William Morris: Romantic to Revolutionary.* 2d ed. New York: Pantheon, 1977.

Thomson, James. *The Seasons.* Ed. James Sambrook. Oxford: Clarendon, 1981.

Tompkins, J. M. S. *William Morris: An Approach to the Poetry.* London: Cecil Woolf, 1988.

Trilling, Lionel. "Aggression and Utopia: A Note on William Morris's *News from Nowhere.*" In *The Last Decade: Essays and Reviews, 1965–75,* ed. Diana Trilling, 148–59. New York: Harcourt Brace Jovanovich, 1979.

Tuveson, Ernest. "The Origins of the 'Moral Sense.'" *Huntington Library Quarterly* 11 (1948): 241–59.

Unger, Roberto Mangabeira. *Knowledge and Politics.* New York: Free Press, 1976.

Unrau, John. "Ruskin, the Workman, and the Savageness of Gothic." In *New Approaches to Ruskin: Thirteen Essays,* ed. Robert Hewison, 33–50. London: Routledge and Kegan Paul, 1981.

Usher, James. *Clio; or, A Discourse on Taste.* 2d ed. London, 1769; New York: Garland, 1970.

Voitle, Robert. "Shaftesbury's Moral Sense." *Studies in Philology* 52 (1955): 17–38.

Watts, G. F. "The Present Conditions of Art." *Nineteenth Century* 7 (Feb. 1880): 235–55.

Weinberg, Gail S. "Ruskin, Pater, and the Rediscovery of Botticelli." *Burlington Magazine* 129 (1987): 25–27.

Wells, H. G. "The Rediscovery of the Unique." *Fortnightly Review* o.s. 56, n.s. 50 (July 1891): 106–11.

Whipple, Edwin Percy. *Recollections of Eminent Men.* Boston: Ticknor, 1886.

Whistler, James Abbott McNeill. *The Gentle Art of Making Enemies.* London, 1892; rpt. New York: Dover, 1967.

White, Gleeson. "Sandro Botticelli (Filipepi)." *Dome* 1 (1897): 81–87.

Wilde, Oscar. *The Artist as Critic: Critical Writings of Oscar Wilde.* Ed. Richard Ellmann. New York: Random House, 1968.

———. *The Complete Works of Oscar Wilde.* Ed. Robert Ross. 10 vols. Boston: Wyman-Fogg, 1908.

———. *The Letters of Oscar Wilde.* Ed. Rupert Hart-Davis. New York: Harcourt Brace and World, 1962.

———. *Oscar Wilde's Oxford Notebooks: A Portrait of Mind in the Making.* Ed. Philip E. Smith and Michael S. Helfand. New York: Oxford Univ. Press, 1989.

———. *The Poetry of Oscar Wilde: A Critical Edition.* Ed. Bobby Fong. 2 vols. Ann Arbor, Mich.: Univ. Microfilms International, 1978.

Williams, Carolyn. *Transfigured World: Walter Pater's Aesthetic Historicism.* Ithaca: Cornell Univ. Press, 1989.

Williams, Raymond. *Culture and Society: 1780–1950.* New York: Columbia Univ. Press, 1983.

Wilson, J. Dover. Introduction to *Culture and Anarchy,* ed. J. Dover Wilson, xi–xl. Cambridge: Cambridge Univ. Press, 1969.

Woodmansee, Martha. *The Author, Art, and the Market: Rereading the History of Aesthetics.* New York: Columbia Univ. Press, 1994.

Yeats, William Butler. *The Autobiography of William Butler Yeats.* New York: Macmillan, 1965.

———. *Memoirs.* Ed. Denis Donoghue. London: Macmillan, 1972.

Young, Helen H. *The Writings of Walter Pater: A Reflection of British Philosophical Opinion from 1860 to 1890.* Bryn Mawr, Pa., 1933; rpt. New York: Haskell, 1965.

Index

Victorian Literature and Culture Series
Karen Chase, Jerome J. McGann, *and* Herbert Tucker, *General Editors*

Daniel Albright
Tennyson: *The Muses' Tug-of-War*

David G. Riede
Matthew Arnold and the Betrayal of Language

Anthony Winner
Culture and Irony: *Studies in Joseph Conrad's Major Novels*

James Richardson
Vanishing Lives: *Style and Self in Tennyson, D. G. Rossetti, Swinburne, and Yeats*

Jerome J. McGann, Editor
Victorian Connections

Antony H. Harrison
Victorian Poets and Romantic Poems: *Intertextuality and Ideology*

E. Warwick Slinn
The Discourse of Self in Victorian Poetry

Linda K. Hughes and Michael Lund
The Victorian Serial

Anna Leonowens
The Romance of the Harem
Edited and with an Introduction by Susan Morgan

Alan Fischler
Modified Rapture: *Comedy in W. S. Gilbert's Savoy Operas*

Barbara Timm Gates, Editor
Journal of Emily Shore, with a new Introduction by the Editor

Richard Maxwell
The Mysteries of Paris and London

Felicia Bonaparte
The Gypsy-Bachelor of Manchester: *The Life of Mrs. Gaskell's Demon*

Peter L. Shillingsburg
Pegasus in Harness: *Victorian Publishing and W. M. Thackeray*

Angela Leighton
Victorian Women Poets: *Writing Against the Heart*

Allan C. Dooley
Author and Printer in Victorian England

Simon Gatrell
Thomas Hardy and the Proper Study of Mankind

Jeffrey Skoblow
Paradise Dislocated: *Morris, Politics, Art*

Matthew Rowlinson
Tennyson's Fixations: *Psychoanalysis and the Topics of the Early Poetry*

Beverly Seaton
The Language of Flowers: *A History*

Barry Milligan
Pleasures and Pains: *Opium and the Orient in Nineteenth-Century British Culture*

Ginger S. Frost
Promises Broken: *Courtship, Class, and Gender in Victorian England*

Linda Dowling
The Vulgarization of Art: *The Victorians and Aesthetic Democracy*